Western Civilization
Primary Source
READER

◇

VOLUME
I

Western Civilization
Primary Source
READER

◇

VOLUME
I

Megan McLean
University of Pittsburgh

Boston   Burr Ridge, IL   Dubuque, IA   Madison, WI   New York   San Francisco   St. Louis
Bangkok   Bogotá   Caracas   Kuala Lumpur   Lisbon   London   Madrid   Mexico City
Milan   Montreal   New Delhi   Santiago   Seoul   Singapore   Sydney   Taipei   Toronto

WESTERN CIVILIZATION PRIMARY SOURCE READER, VOLUME I
Published by McGraw-Hill, a business unit of The McGraw-Hill Companies, Inc., 1221
Avenue of the Americas, New York, NY, 10020. Copyright © 2003 by The McGraw-Hill
Companies, Inc. All rights reserved. No part of this publication may be reproduced or
distributed in any form or by any means, or stored in a database or retrieval system,
without prior written consent of The McGraw-Hill Companies, Inc., including, but not
limited to, in any network or other electronic storage or transmission, or broadcast for
distance learning.

1 2 3 4 5 6 7 8 9 0 FGR/FGR 0 9 8 7 6 5 4 3 2

ISBN 0-07-283722-5

Vice president and editor-in-chief: *Thalia Dorwick*
Executive editor: *Lyn Uhl*
Sponsoring editor: *Monica Eckman*
Editorial coordinator: *Angela Kao*
Marketing manager: *Katherine Bates*
Project manager: *Marc Mattson/Susan Trentacosti*
Production supervisor: *Carol Bielski*
Permissions editor: *Marty Granahan*
Cover design: *Marc Mattson*
Compositor: *Todd Sanders*

Cover photo (detail): © *Art Resource, NY*

www.mhhe.com

CONTENTS

INTRODUCTION   vii

CHAPTER 1   *The Epic of Gilgamesh*   3
                 The Book of the Dead   13

CHAPTER 2   Herodotus, *The Histories*   27
                 Plato, *Apology of Socrates*   37

CHAPTER 3   Arrian, *The Life of Alexander the Great*   49

CHAPTER 4   Virgil, *Aeneid*   61
                 Strabo, *The Geography of Strabo*   73

CHAPTER 5   Josephus, *The Antiquities of the Jews*   83
                 Egeria, *Diary of a Pilgrimage*   99

CHAPTER 6   ʿAlī ibn Ridwān, *On the Prevention of Bodily Ills in Egypt*   109

CHAPTER 7   Einhard, *The Life of Charlemagne*   119
                 Dhuoda, *Handbook for William*   127

CHAPTER 8   Ramón Lull, *Felix*   141

CHAPTER 9   Marco Polo, *The Travels of Marco Polo*   151
                 Boccaccio, *The Decameron*   161

CHAPTER 10   Giovanni Pico della Mirandola, *On the Dignity of Man*   173

CHAPTER 11   Erasmus, *The Handbook of the Militant Christian*   183
                 Jacob Sprenger and Heinrich Kramer,   193
                 Malleus Maleficarum

CHAPTER 12   Bartolomé de las Casas, *The Devastation of the Indies*   203

CHAPTER 13   Madame de Lafayette, *The Princess of Clèves*   213
                 John Locke, *Second Treatise of Government*   223

CHAPTER 14   Baron de Montesquieu, *The Persian Letters*   237
                 Rousseau, *The Social Contract*   247

CREDITS   255

INTRODUCTION

The primary source documents compiled in this volume are intended
to accompany and supplement the narrative treatment of themes that most
Western civilization textbooks provide. These sources were chosen to give
voice to individuals who observed first hand the birth and evolution of
Western civilization. The observations recorded in these documents bring
to life the social, cultural, economic, and political trends that have shaped
the course of Western civilization by giving students insight into how
diverse individuals participated in and reacted to these transformations.
Some of the historical personalities included here will no doubt be
familiar to students; others are less well known because they viewed these
trends and transformations from the margins of Western civilization. Yet
all contribute to our understanding of the role of human agency in shaping
historical developments.

Instructors may wish to use these sources as supplemental readings
to a textbook, or as tools for encouraging classroom discussions. The
documents could provide the basis for writing or research assignments.
Many of the documents overlap slightly in terms of time periods and
themes, and instructors may wish to employ two or three documents at a
time to stimulate discussions of the diversity of experiences of a particular
event or trend. Each document is preceded by a brief introduction. That
introduction outlines the life of the author against the background of the
major historical trends that likely influenced his or her work. Then the
themes addressed by the author in the excerpted work are summarized,
and the specific passage is introduced. A few discussion questions at the
end of each introduction encourage students to analyze the sources
critically in light of broader historical changes. Lastly, the source listings
provide additional biographical and critical cites for the individual author
and his or her work.

Megan McLean
University of Pittsburgh

CHAPTER 1

The Epic of Gilgamesh

The Book of the Dead

THE EPIC OF GILGAMESH

Between 3000 and 1000 B.C., people developed a sophisticated society in the region called Mesopotamia, a valley lying between the Tigris and Euphrates rivers. These people, the Sumerians, coped with the unpredictable nature of their environment by organizing complex social hierarchies in which the priests provided guidance and order. The Sumerians made impressive advances in many areas: their city-states, public law codes, and advances in astronomy and mathematics set new standards of civilization among the ancient societies of the Fertile Crescent. The religious beliefs of these innovative people reflected the harsh conditions that they struggled to overcome. Their deities acted capriciously, while demons also required appeasement. The Sumerians also embraced a pessimistic vision of the afterlife, in which the dead suffered or beleaguered the living.

The historical Gilgamesh ruled the city of Uruk in Sumer around 2700 B.C. This king was worshipped as a semi-divine hero, and his exploits were eventually glorified in a series of tales that first written down in cuneiform around 2100 B.C. The invention of cuneiform script marked one of the most profound achievements of the Sumerians, who developed this form of writing primarily to record commercial transactions and religious matters. Several versions of the poem have survived. The author of this version of the epic lived around 1300 B.C., and wove the various tales concerning Gilgamesh into a unified epic poem.

The poem recounts the quest of Gilgamesh, first for fame, and then after the death of his beloved companion Enkidu, for immortality. After defeating the demon Humbaba, the Gilgamesh refuse the advances of the goddess Ishtar. Enfuriated at the rejection, Ishtar calls upon her father to send the Bull of Heaven as punishment. Her father, the god Anu, complies, but Gilgamesh and Enkidu triumph and kill the Bull. As punishment for tampering with the will of the gods, a council of wrathful deities decides that one of the men must die. Enkidu is chosen, and Gilgamesh passes the rest of the poem grief-stricken and desperate to recover his friend while avoiding an encounter with his own mortality. The passage below recounts the encounter between Ishtar and Gilgamesh, the battle of with the Bull of Heaven, and the short-lived celebration of the heroes at their victory.

GILGAMESH

Tablet VI

Column i

He washed his grimy hair and cleaned his straps;   1
he shook out the braid of his hair against his back;
he threw off his filthy clothes and put on clean ones;
he covered himself with a cloak, fastened the sash;
Gilgamesh put on his crown.

To Gilgamesh's beauty great Ishtar lifted her eyes.
"Come, Gilgamesh, be my lover!
Give me the taste of your body.   8
Would that you were my husband, and I your wife!
I'd order harnessed for you a chariot of lapis lazuli and gold,
its wheels of gold and its horns of precious amber.
You will drive storm demons-powerful mules!
Enter our house, into the sweet scent of cedarwood.
As you enter our house
the purification priests will kiss your feet the way they do in Aratta.   15
Kings, rulers, princes will bend down before you.
Mountains and lands will bring their yield to you.   17
Your goats will drop triplets, your ewes twins.
Even loaded down, your donkey will overtake the mule.
Your horses will win fame for their running.
Your ox under its yoke will have no rival."

Gilgamesh shaped his mouth to speak,
saying to great Ishtar:
"What could I give you if I should take you as a wife?
Would I give you oil for the body, and fine wrappings?   25
Would I give you bread and victuals?—
you who eat food of the gods,
you who drink wine fit for royalty?
. . .

[For you] they pour out [libations];
[you are clothed with the Great] Garment.
[Ah,] the gap [between us], if I take you in marriage!

You're a cooking fire that goes out in the cold,
a back door that keeps out neither wind nor storm,
a palace that crushes the brave ones defending it,
a well whose lid collapses,
pitch that defiles the one carrying it,
a waterskin that soaks the one who lifts it,
limestone that crumbles in the stone wall,
a battering ram that shatters in the land of the enemy,
a shoe that bites the owner's foot!

Which of your lovers have you loved forever?
Which of your little shepherds has continued to please you?   43
Come, let me name your lovers for you."   44

Column ii

". . .   45
for Tammuz, the lover of your youth.   46
Year after year you set up a wailing for him.
You loved the mauve-colored shepherd bird: 48
you seized him and broke his wing.
In the forest he stands crying, 'Kappi! My wing!'   50
You loved the lion, full of spry power;
you dug for him seven pits and seven pits.   52
You loved the stallion glorious in battle:
you ordained for him the whip, the goad, the halter.
You brought it about that he runs seven leagues;
you brought it about that he roils the water as he drinks.
For his mother, Silili, you gave cause for weeping.
You loved a shepherd, a herdsman,
who endlessly put up cakes for you
and every day slaughtered kids for you.

You struck him, turned him into a wolf.
His own boys drove him away,
and his dogs tore his hide to bits.

You loved also Ishullanu, your father's gardener,   64
who endlessly brought you baskets of dates
and every day made the table jubilant.
You lifted your eyes to him and went to him:
'My Ishullanu, let us take pleasure in your strength.
Reach out your hand and touch my vulva!'
Ishullanu said to you,
'What do you want from me?
Mother, if you don't cook, I don't eat.
Should I eat the bread of bad faith, the food of curses?
Should I be covered with rushes against the cold?'
You heard his answer.
You struck him, turned him into a frog.
You set him to dwell in the middle of the garden,
where he can move neither upward nor downward.

So you'd love me in my turn and, as with them, set my fate."

When Ishtar heard this
Ishtar was furious and flew up to the heavens
and went before Anu the father.
Before Antum, her mother, she wept.   83
"Father, Gilgamesh has insulted me."   84

Column iii

"Gilgamesh has spoken to me of bad faith,   85
my bad faith and my cursings."

Anu shaped his mouth to speak
and said to glorious Ishtar,
"Come, come. Didn't you yourself pick a fight with Gilgamesh,

and Gilgamesh recited your iniquities,
your bad faith and your cursings?"

Ishtar shaped her mouth, speaking,
saying to Anu the father,
"Father, make the Bull of Heaven. Let him kill Gilgamesh in
    the very place he lives;   94
let the bull glut himself on Gilgamesh.
If you do not give me the bull, I will smash in the gates of
the netherworld;   97
I will set up the [ruler] of the great below,
and I will make the dead rise, and they will devour the living,
and the dead will increase beyond the number of the living."

Anu shaped his mouth to speak to glorious Ishtar: 101/2
"If you ask me for the bull,
for seven years the land of Uruk will harvest only chaff.   104
Have you stored up grain for the people?
Have you grown grass for the animals?"

Ishtar shaped her mouth to speak,
saying to Anu the father:
"I have stored up grain for the people.
For the animals I have caused grass to be, for the animals.
If there must be seven years of chaff,
I have stored grain for the people;
I have provided grass for the animals.
. . . to him.
. . .
. . . of the bull."

Anu listened to the words of Ishtar.
[He created for her the Bull of Heaven (?)]
Ishtar drove [him (?) down to earth (?)]
. . . [approaching Uruk.]
. . .
He descends to the river . . .
At the snorting of the bull, a hole opened up:
two hundred of the men of Uruk fell into it.   124

Column iv

. . . men.   125
At his second snorting a hole opened up: two hundred men
fell into it.
Two hundred men . . . three hundred men . . .
Even three hundred men of Uruk fell into it, *etc.*   128
At the third snorting a hole opened before Enkidu.
Enkidu fell upon him.
Enkidu leaped up, seized the Bull of Heaven, took hold of
    his horns.
The Bull of Heaven threw spittle into Enkidu's face;   132
he threw excrement on him.

Enkidu shaped his mouth, speaking,
saying to Gilgamesh:
"Friend, we have made ourselves great . . .
How shall we overthrow him?
Friend, I see . . .
and strength . . .
Let us destroy . . .
I . . .
Let us be strong . . .
Let us fill . . .
. . .
and stick him behind the neck."   145
. . .
Enkidu circles him, chasing the Bull of Heaven.
He seized him and [threw his excrement],
. . .   149

Column v

And Gilgamesh, like a matador . . .   150
mighty and . . .
struck [with his sword] in the neck [behind the horns].

9

After they had killed the Bull they tore out his heart.
They set it before Shamash. 154
They withdrew and worshipped Shamash.
They sat down, blood-brothers, the two of them. 156

Ishtar went up on the walls of Uruk of the Sheepfold.
Disguised as a mourner she let loose a curse:
"Curse Gilgamesh, who has besmeared me, killing the Bull
of Heaven!"

When Enkidu heard this, the words of Ishtar,
he tore out the thigh of the bull and threw it in her face. 161
"If I could reach you, as I can him,
it would have been done to you: 163
I'd hang his guts around your arm!"

Ishtar called together the hair-curled high priestesses, 165
the love-priestesses and temple whores,
and over the thigh of the Bull of Heaven she set up a wailing.

Gilgamesh called together [the city's] experts, the craftsmen,
all of them.
Young specialists examined the thickness of the horns.
Each was made of thirty minas of lapis lazuli,
and the plating of each was two fingers thick.
The capacity of the two was six measures of oil,
which he offered as a lotion to his god Lugalbanda. 174
He brought [the horns] in and hung them in the shrine of his
ancestors. 175
They washed their hands in the Euphrates.
They embraced each other as they walked along.

Mounted they rode through the streets of Uruk,
and the people of Uruk gathered to look up at them.
Gilgamesh speaks these words to the people assembled,
to the women he says: 181

Column vi

"Who is the best formed of heroes?   182
Who is the most powerful among men?
Gilgamesh is the best formed of heroes.
[Enkidu is] the most powerful among men.
. . . our strength
. . . [the final investment of lordship they have not.]
. . . [seal of] . . . [sickness].
In his palace Gilgamesh holds a joyful celebration.
[At last] the heroes lie down, sleeping at night in their beds.
Enkidu, lying down, sees dreams.
Enkidu jerked upright to set free the dream,
saying to his friend:

————

"Friend, why are the great gods in council?"   193

Discussion Questions

1. What kinds of rewards does Ishtar offer Gilgamesh in her
   proposal of marriage to him? Why does Gilgamesh reject Ishtar's
   proposal?

2. How are gods and humans portrayed in this fragment of the
   poem? What divides the divine from the human?

Sources

Gilgamesh, trans. John Gardner and John Maier, with Richard A.
    Henshaw, New York: Alfred A. Knopf, 1984.

The Epic of Gilgamesh, trans. Maureen Gallery Kovacs, Stanford:
    Stanford University Press, 1989.

THE BOOK
OF THE DEAD

Unlike the dark and unpleasant afterworld envisioned by the Mesopotamians, the ancient Egyptians imagined a pleasant afterlife. They developed complex funereal rites to increase the chances that their dead would journey safely through the treacherous underworld to heaven. To improve the chances of the dead person, the Egyptians inscribed prayers and drawings on the walls of tombs, directly on coffins, or on sheets of papyrus. These spells appealed to the gods to protect the dead from the dangers that he or she would encounter in their travels from this world to the next.

The papyri from which scholars have compiled *The Book of the Dead* date from mid-fifteenth century B.C. However, the prayers probably originated earlier and were passed down orally over the centuries. These prayers were initially intended to ensure that royal leaders, considered divine, enjoyed the fruits of the afterlife. The democratization of access to the afterlife and funeral rites themselves during the Middle Kingdom led to the proliferation of different spells. These texts incorporated traditions from earlier kingdoms, such as the importance of the sun god Re, beliefs that the dead would ascend to rest among the stars, and homage to Osiris, one of the Nile spirits. Scribes created individualized prayers for affluent individuals, who could sometimes afford to purchase the entire repertoire of spells. People of more humble origins purchased a few prayers copied without variation from the scribes' master books. They were written in hieroglyphic signs, usually with black ink, but sometimes with red or yellow highlights.

The spells below date from the New Kingdom, approximately 1570-1085 B.C.

These texts come from the beginning of *The Book of the Dead,* in which the bearer prepares to emerge from his or her tomb the day after burial. The first sections are addressed to Re or Osiris; later ones declare the innocence of the dead before the gates of justice or a tribunal of judges. If these lists of behavior are any indication, the Egyptians clearly valued generosity, honesty, and respect for other human beings.

THE BOOK OF THE DEAD

Introductory Hymn to the Sun God Re

WORSHIP OF RE WHEN HE RISES IN THE EASTERN HORIZON OF THE SKY BY N

He says: Hail to you, you having come as Khepri, even Khepri who is the creator of the gods. You rise and shine on the back of your mother (the sky), having appeared in glory as King of the gods. Your mother Nut shall use her arms on your behalf in making greeting. The Manumountain receives you in peace, Maat embraces you at all seasons. May you give power and might in vindication—and a coming forth as a living soul to see Horakhty—to the ka of N.

He says: O all you gods of the Soul-mansion who judge sky and earth in the balance, who give food and provisions; O Tatenen, Unique One, creator of mankind; O Southern, Northern, Western and Eastern Enneads, give praise to Re, Lord of the Sky, the Sovereign who made the gods. Worship him in his goodly shape when he appears in the Day-bark. May those who are above worship you, may those who are below worship you, may Thoth and Maat write to you daily; your serpent-foe has been given over to the fire and the rebel-serpent is fallen, his arms are bound, Re has taken away his movements, and the Children of Impotence are nonexistent. The Mansion of the Prince is in festival, the noise of shouting is in the Great Place, the gods are in joy, when they see Re in his appearing, his rays flooding the lands. The Majesty of this noble god proceeds, he has entered the land of Manu, the land is bright at his daily birth, and he has attained his state of yesterday. May you be gracious to me when I see your beauty, having departed from upon earth. May I smite the Ass, may I drive off the rebel-serpent, may I destroy Apep when he acts, for I have seen the abdju-fish in its moment of being and the bulti-fish piloting the canoe on its waterway. I have seen Horus as helmsman, with Thoth and Maat beside him, I have taken hold of the bow-warp of the Night-bark and the stern-warp of the Day-bark. May he grant that I see the sun-disc and behold the moon unceasingly every day; may my soul go forth to travel to every place which it desires; may my name be called out, may

it be found at the board of offerings; may there be given to me loaves
in the Presence like the Followers of Horus, may a place be made for
me in the solar bark on the day when the god ferries across, and may I
be received into the presence of Osiris in the Land of Vindication.

For the ka of N.

Introductory Hymn to Osiris

WORSHIP of Osiris Wennefer, the Great God who dwells in the Thinite
nome, King of Eternity, Lord of Everlasting, who passes millions of
years in his lifetime first-born son of Nut, begotten of Geb, Heir, Lord
of the Wereret-crown, whose White Crown is tall, Sovereign of gods
and men. He has taken the crook and the flail and the office of his
forefathers. May your heart which is in the desert land be glad, for your
son Horus is firm on your throne, while you have appeared as Lord of
Busiris, as the Ruler who is in Abydos. The Two Lands flourish in
vindication because of you in the presence of the Lord of All. All that
exists is ushered in to him in his name of 'Face to whom men are
ushered'; the Two Lands are marshalled for him as leader in this his
name of Sokar; his might is far-reaching, one greatly feared in this his
name of Osiris; he passes over the length of eternity in his name of
Wennefer.

Hail to you, King of Kings, Lord of Lords, Ruler of Rulers, who took
possession of the Two Lands even in the womb of Nut; he rules the
plains of the Silent Land, even he the golden of body, blue of head, on
whose arms is turquoise. O Pillar of Myriads, broad of breast, kindly of
countenance, who is in the Sacred Land: May you grant power in the
sky, might on earth and vindication in the realm of the dead, a
journeying downstream to Busiris as a living soul and a journeying
upstream to Abydos as a heron; to go in and out without hindrance at
all the gates of the Netherworld. May there be given to me bread from
the House of Cool Water and a table of offerings from Heliopolis, my
toes being firm-planted in the Field of Rushes. May the barley and
emmer which are in it belong to the ka of the Osiris N.

The Judgement of the Dead

THE HEART OF THE DEAD MAN IS WEIGHED IN THE SCALES OF THE BALANCE AGAINST THE FEATHER OF RIGHTEOUSNESS

SPELL 3OB

O my heart which I had from my mother! O my heart which I had from my mother! O my heart of my different ages! Do not stand up as a witness against me, do not be opposed to me in the tribunal, do not be hostile to me in the presence of the Keeper of the Balance, for you are my ka which was in my body, the protector who made my members hale. Go forth to the happy place whereto we speed; do not make my name stink to the Entourage who make men, Do not tell lies about

SPELL 125

INTRODUCTION

What should be said when arriving at this Hall of Justice, purging N of all the evil which he has done, and beholding the faces of the gods

Hail to you, great god, Lord of Justice! I have come to you, my lord, that you may bring me so that I may see your beauty, for I know you and I know your name, and I know the names of the forty-two gods of those who are with you in this Hall of Justice, who live on those who cherish evil and who gulp down their blood on that day of the reckoning of characters in the presence of Wennefer. Behold the double son of the Songstresses; Lord of Truth is your name. Behold, I have come to you, I have brought you truth, I have repelled falsehood for you. I have not done falsehood against men, I have not impoverished my associates, I have done no wrong in the Place of Truth, I have not learnt that which is not, I have done no evil, I have not daily made labour in excess of what was due to be done for me, my name has not reached the offices of those who control slaves, I have not deprived the orphan of his property, I have not done what the gods detest, I have not calumniated a servant to his master, I have not caused pain, I have not made hungry, I have not made to weep, I have not killed, I have not commanded to kill, I have not made suffering for anyone, I have not lessened the food-offerings in the temples, I have not destroyed the loaves of the gods, I have not taken away the food of the spirits, I have not copulated, I have not misbehaved, I have not lessened food-supplies, I have not diminished the aroura, I have not encroached upon fields, I have not laid anything upon the weights of the hand-balance, I have not taken anything from the plummet of the standing scales, I have not taken the milk from the mouths of children, I have not deprived the herds of their pastures, I have not trapped the birds from the preserves of the gods, I have not caught the fish of their marshlands, I have not diverted water at its season, I have not built a dam on flowing water, I have not quenched the fire when it is burning, I have not neglected the dates for offering choice meats, I have not withheld cattle from the god's-offerings, I have not opposed a god in his procession.

I am pure, pure, pure, pure! My purity is the purity of that great phoenix which is in Heracleopolis, because I am indeed the nose of the Lord of Wind who made all men live on that day of completing the Sacred Eye in Heliopolis *in the 2nd month of winter last day,* in the presence of the lord of this land. I am he who saw the completion of the Sacred Eye in Heliopolis, and nothing evil shall come into being against me in this land in this Hall of Justice, because I know the names of these gods who are in it.

THE DECLARATION OF INNOCENCE BEFORE THE GODS
OF THE TRIBUNAL

O Far-strider who came forth from Heliopolis, I have done no falsehood.

O Fire-embracer who came forth from Kheraha, I have not robbed.

O Nosey who came forth from Hermopolis, I have not been rapacious.

O Swallower of shades who came forth from the cavern, I have not stolen.

O Dangerous One who came forth from Rosetjau, I have not killed men.

O Double Lion who came forth from the sky, I have not destroyed food-supplies.

O Fiery Eyes who came forth from Letopolis, I have done no crookedness.

O   Flame which came forth backwards, I have not stolen the god's-offerings.

O   Bone-breaker who came forth from Heracleopolis, I have not told lies.

O   Green of flame who came forth from Memphis, I have not taken food.

O   You of the cavern who came forth from the West, I have not been sullen.

O   White of teeth who came forth from the Faiyum, I have not transgressed.

O   Blood-eater who came forth from the shambles, I have not killed a sacred bull.

O   Eater of entrails who came forth from the House of Thirty, I have not committed perjury.

O   Lord of Truth who came forth from Maaty, I have not stolen bread.

O   Wanderer who came forth from Bubastis, I have not eavesdropped.

O   Pale One who came forth from Heliopolis, I have not babbled.

O   Doubly evil who came forth from Andjet, I have not disputed except as concerned my own property.

O   Wememty-snake who came forth from the place of execution, I have not committed homosexuality.

O   You who see whom you bring who came forth from the House of Mm, I have not misbehaved.

O   You who are over the Old One who came forth from Imau, I have not made terror.

O   Demolisher who came forth from Xois, I have not transgressed.

O   Disturber who came forth from Weryt, I have not been hot-tempered.

O   Youth who came forth from the Heliopolitan nome, I have not been deaf to words of truth.

O   Foreteller who came forth from Wenes, I have not made disturbance.

O   You of the altar who came forth from the secret place, I have not hoodwinked.

O   You whose face is behind him who came forth from the Cavern of Wrong, I have neither misconducted myself nor copulated with a boy.

O   Hot-foot who came forth from the dusk, I have not been neglectful.

O   You of the darkness who came forth from the darkness, I have not been quarrelsome.

O   Bringer of your offering who came forth from Sais, I have not been unduly active.

O   Owner of faces who came forth from Nedjefet, I have not been impatient.

O   Accuser who came forth from Wetjenet, I have not transgressed my nature, I have not washed out (the picture of) a god.

O   Owner of horns who came forth from Asyut, I have not been voluble in speech.

O   Nefertum who came forth from Memphis, I have done no wrong, I have seen no evil.

O   Temsep who came forth from Busiris, I have not made conjuration against the king.

O   You who acted according to your will, who came forth from Tjebu, I have not waded in water.

O   Water-smiter who came forth from the Abyss, I have not been loud voiced.

O   Commander of mankind who came forth from your house, I have not reviled God.

O   Bestower of good who came forth from the Harpoon nome, I have not done . . .

O   Bestower of powers who came forth from the City, I have not made distinctions for myself.

O   Serpent with raised head who came forth from the cavern, I am not wealthy except with my own property.

O   Serpent who brings and gives, who came forth from the Silent Land, I have not blasphemed God in my city.

ADDRESS TO THE GOD OF THE HALL OF JUSTICE

Thus says N: Hail to you, you gods who are in this Hall of Justice! I know you and I know your names, I will not fall to your knives; you shall not bring the evil in me to this god in whose suite you are, no fault of mine concerning you shall come out, you shall tell the truth about me in the presence of the Lord of All, because I have done what was right in Egypt, I have not reviled God, and no fault of mine has come out regarding the reigning king.

Hail to you, O you who are in the Hall of Justice, who have no lies in your bodies, who live on truth and gulp down truth in the presence of Horus who is in his disc. Save me from Babai, who lives on the entrails of the old ones on that day of the great reckoning. Behold, I have come to you without falsehood of mine, without crime of mine, without evil of mine, and there is no one who testifies against me, for I have done nothing against him. I live on truth, I gulp down truth, I have done what men say and with which the gods are pleased. I have propitiated God with what he desires; I have given bread to the hungry, water to the thirsty, clothes to the naked and a boat to him who was boatless, I have given god's-offerings to the gods and invocation-offerings to the spirits. Save me, protect me, without your making report against me in the Presence, for I am pure of mouth and pure of hands, one to whom is said 'Twice welcome!' by those who see him, because I have heard that great word which the noble dead spoke with the Cat in the House of Him whose mouth gapes. He who testifies of me is He whose face is behind him, and he gives the cry. I have seen the dividing of the ished-tree in Rosetjau, I am he who succours the gods, who knows the affairs of their bodies. I have come here to bear witness to truth and to set the balance in its proper place within the Silent Land.

O You who are uplifted on your standard, Lord of the Atef-crown, who made your name as Lord of the Wind, save me from your messengers who shoot forth harm and create punishments and who show no indulgence, because I have done what is right for the Lord of Right. I am pure, my brow is clean, my hinder-parts are cleansed, and my middle is in the Pool of Truth, there is no member in me devoid of truth. I have bathed in the Southern Pool, I have rested in the Northern City, in the pure Field of Grasshoppers, in which is the crew of Re, in this second hour of the night and the third hour of the day, and the gods are calmed when they pass by it by night or by day.

THE DEAD MAN IS QUESTIONED

'You have caused him to come,' say they about me. 'Who are you?' they say to me. 'What is your name?' they say to me.

'I am the lower part of the papyrus-plant; "He who is on his moringa-tree" is my name. 'What have you passed by?' they say to me.'

'I have passed by the city north of the moringatree.'

'What did you see there?'

'They were the calf and the thigh.'

'What did you say to them?'

'I have seen the rejoicings in these lands of the Fenkhu.'

'What did they give you?'

'A fire-brand and a pillar of faience.'

'What did you do with them?'

'I buried them on the river-bank of Maat with the night-ritual.'

'What did you find on it, the river-bank of Maat?'

'It was a staff of flint called "Giver of Breath".'

'What did you do with the fire-brand and the pillar of faience after you had buried them?'

'I called out over them, I dug them up, I quenched the fire, I broke the pillar and threw it into a canal.'

'Come and enter by this door of the Hall of Justice, for you know us.'

'We will not let you enter by us,' say the door-posts of this door,'unless you tell our name.'

'"Plummet of Truth" is your name.'

'I will not let you enter by me,' says the right-hand leaf of this door, 'unless you tell my name.'

'"Scale-pan which weighs Truth" is your name.'

'I will not let you enter by me,' says the left-hand leaf of this door, 'unless you tell my name.'

'"Scale-pan of wine" is your name.'

'I will not let you pass by me,' says the floor of this door, 'unless you tell my name.'

'"Ox of Geb" is your name.'

'I will not open to you,' says the door-bolt of this door, 'unless you tell my name.'

'"Toe of his mother" is your name.'

'I will not let you enter by me,' says the hasp of this door, 'unless you tell my name.'

'"Living Eye of Sobk, Lord of Bakhu" is your name.'

'I will not open to you,' says this door, 'unless you tell my name.'

'"Breast of Shu which he placed as a protection for Osiris" is your name.'

'We will not let you enter by us,' say the crosstimbers, 'unless you tell our names.'

'"Children of uraei" are your names.'

'I will not open to you nor let you enter by me,' says the door-keeper of this door, 'unless you tell my name.'

'"Ox of Geb" is your name.'

'You know us; pass by us.'

'I will not let you tread on me,' says the floor of this Hall of Justice.

'Why not? I am pure.'

'Because I do not know the names of your feet with which you would tread on me. Tell them to me.'

'"Secret image of Ha" is the name of my right foot; "Flower of Hathor" is the name of my left foot."'

'You know us; enter by us.'

'I will not announce you,' says the door-keeper of this Hall of Justice, 'unless you tell my name.'

'"Knower of hearts, searcher-out of bodies" is your name.'

'To which god shall I announce you?'

'To him who is now present. Tell it to the Dragoman of the Two Lands.'

'Who is the Dragoman of the Two Lands?'

'He is Thoth.'

'Come!' says Thoth. 'What have you come for?'

'I have come here to report.'

'What is your condition?'

'I am pure from evil, I have excluded myself from the quarrels of those who are now living, I am not among them.'

'To whom shall I announce you?'

'You shall announce me to Him whose roof is fire, whose walls are living uraei, the floor of whose house is the waters.'

'Who is he?'

'He is Osiris.'

'Proceed; behold, you are announced. Your bread is the Sacred Eye, your beer is the Sacred Eye; what goes forth at the voice for you upon earth is the Sacred Eye.'

Discussion Questions

1. What kinds of appeals are made by the dead to the gods Re and Osiris?

2. What, for the Egyptians, makes a person worthy of entering heaven? How did they define purity and innocence?

Sources

The Ancient Egyptian Book of the Dead, trans. Raymond O. Faulkner, London: British Museum Publications, 1985.

E.A. Wallis Budge, *The Book of the Dead*, London, Boston, Melbourne and Henley: ARKANA, 1985.

CHAPTER 2

Herodotus
The Histories

Plato
Apology of Socrates

HERODOTUS ON EGYPT FROM *THE HISTORIES*

Herodotus, a native of Halicarnassus, a Greek city in southwestern Turkey, was born around 484 B.C. to a privileged family of Greek citizenry but of non-Greek origins. As a young man, Herodotus participated in a coup against the tyrant Lygdamis and was exiled to the island of Samos. A second coup in which the young writer also played a part succeeded in expelling the ruler, and Herodotus returned to his home. However, soon after, he began to travel extensively, visiting much of Greece, the eastern Mediterranean, and Egypt. In the mid-400s B.C., Greeks were free to move around the territory of their former enemy, the Persians. At the end of his life, he migrated to city of Thurioi in southern Italy around 444 B.C. where he became a citizen in the newly founded colony. He likely witnessed the early years of the Peloponnesian War, which would lead eventually to Greece's demise.

Herodotus' life spanned the victory of the Greeks over Persia and the flowering of culture and the arts as well as the spread of democracy that accompanied Athens' preeminence among the Greek states. His histories, composed of nine books, covered the origins and causes of the conflict between Greece and Persia, which had climaxed around 480 B.C., early in Herodotus' life. Herodotus is often credited with being the father of modern history, but he has also been considered a gifted storyteller, a moralist, and in a sense, a precursor of the modern journalist because he tried to chronicle events that had taken place in the recent past. In an effort to distinguish between myth and history, the Greek writer sought facts through oral histories compiled during his extensive travels. The histories recount the tale of an era, in which rational and human causes rather than supernatural ones explain the conflict.

Before delving into the conflict between Greece and Persia, Herodotus provided a survey of the world known to the Greek citizen at the time. The histories, in an effort to demonstrate the epic proportions of that conflict and its effect on the Mediterranean world, range over a vast array of subject matter as diverse as geography, ethnographic descriptions of customs, religion, and warfare, and natural history. In the following passage, Herodotus describes the social customs and religion of Egypt. He finds tremendous parallels between the practices of the Egyptians and the Greeks. Herodotus identifies many of the Egyptian deities by their Greek counterparts, claiming that many of these religious entities and customs were transmitted from Egypt to Greece.

35. But of Egypt I shall have much to say, because that country far surpasses all others in marvels, nor can works so inexpressibly great be seen elsewhere: for that reason I shall describe it fully.

Just as the climate of Egypt and its river differ from all others, so the customs and laws of the Egyptians are contrary to those of other men in almost all respects. Among them the women go to market and do business: the men stay at home and weave. And whereas in weaving other peoples push the woof upwards, they push it down. Men carry burdens on their heads, women on their shoulders. The women make water standing, the men crouching. The Egyptians discharge their excrements at home and eat outside in the streets, maintaining that unseemly needs should be attended to in private, but those that are not unseemly in public. No woman is a minister of any deity, whether male or female: all are served by men. Sons are not constrained against their will to maintain their parents; but daughters, however unwilling, must do so.

36. In other countries the priests of the gods wear their hair: in Egypt they are shaven. In mourning it is customary among other peoples for those most nearly concerned to shave their heads; the Egyptians, who are close shaven at other times, let the hair on their heads and faces grow after a death. Other men live separated from their beasts: in Egypt man and beast live together. Other nations use wheat and barley for food: in Egypt it is a great reproach to do so; they make bread from *olyra*. They knead dough with their feet, but they will pick up mud and dung in their hands. Other peoples leave their private parts in the natural state; but the Egyptians and those who have learned from them are circumcised. Men wear two garments: women but one. Other men make the gear of their sails fast to the outsides of ships: the Egyptians to the insides. In writing and calculating with pebbles the Greeks move their hands from left to right: the Egyptians from right toleft. Yet they say that in so doing they work towards the right and the Greeks to the left. They have two sorts of writing, one called sacred and the other common.

37. They are extremely devout, far more so than any other people. They have these customs. They drink from cups of bronze, and wash

them every day: not some but all do this. They wear linen garments, and are very careful always to have them newly-washed. It is for cleanliness that they practise circumcision, valuing cleanliness above comeliness. The priests shave all parts of their bodies once in three days, for fear lest when they serve the gods they might have lice or other foulness about them. The priests wear none but linen garments and sandals of papyrus: other kinds of clothing or sandals are forbidden them. They wash in cold water twice every day and twice every night; and their religious customs are so many that you must count them by tens of thousands. On the other hand, they enjoy great advantages: they consume and spend nothing of their own, consecrated food is cooked for them, and each of them is furnished every day with beef andgeese in abundance and wine made from the grape. Fish they may not eat. Beans are never sown in Egypt, and if any chance to grow, the Egyptians will not eat them raw or cooked; the priests even abhor the sight of them, accounting them unclean. The service of every god is performed not by one priest but by many, of whom one is the arch-priest; and when one priest dies, his place is taken by his son.

38. They regard bulls as belonging to Apis, and they examine them to see whether they have so much as one black hair: if so, they are accounted unclean. One of the priests, appointed for this work, views every part of the animal, both standing and lying, and he pulls out the tongue to see that it bears none of the marks that I shall describe hereafter. Last he looks at the hairs of the tail to make sure that they grow as they ought. If the bull be unblemished in all these respects, the priest marks it by wrapping papyrus round the horns, which he smears with sealing-earth and stamps with his signet-ring. Then it is led away. For sacrificing a beast that the priest has not certified the penalty is death. Such is the examination of the animal: now for the manner of the sacrifice.

39. After bringing the marked victim to the altar where they are going to sacrifice, they kindle fire, and pouring wine over the victim and calling upon the god, they slit the throat and then cut the head off. The body is flayed and the head is cursed much and taken away. If there be a market and Greek traders are to be found there, they take the head to the market for sale: otherwise they throw it in the river. The curse that they utter over the head is that all the ills that threaten those sacrificing and Egypt in general may be averted and fall on this

head. This cursing of the head and pouring of wine are customary in all Egyptian sacrifices; and because of the custom no Egyptian will taste of the head of any animal.

40. But as to the cleaning out and burning of the victim there are different customs for various kinds of sacrifice. I will describe those made to her whom they regard as highest of all and to whom they pay the greatest honours. When they have flayed the bull and prayed, they take out the lower entrails, leaving the upper entrails and the fat in the carcase. Then they cut off the legs, the end of the loin, the shoulders and the neck, and having filled the body with fine bread, honey, raisins, frankincense, myrrh and other spices, they offer it up, pouring on abundance of oil. They fast before the sacrifice, and whilst it is burning they utter lamentations: afterwards they cease from mourning and set forth a feast of the remains of the offering.

41. All the Egyptians sacrifice unblemished bulls and bull-calves; but cows they may not, for these are sacred to Isis. For the image of Isis is always made in the form of a woman with the horns of an ox, as Io is pictured by the Greeks; and for that reason all Egyptians are alike in treating cows as far more holy than any other beasts. For that reason also no Egyptian man or woman will kiss a Greek on the mouth, nor will they use a knife or spit or cooking-pot belonging to a Greek, or even taste of the flesh of an unblemished bull that has been cut with a Greek's knife. When a beast of this kind dies naturally, they dispose of the body in this way: they throw cows in the river, and the males they bury in the outskirts of the cities with one or both of the horns showing to mark the grave. Then, when the flesh is decomposed, in due time a boat comes to each city from the island called Prosopitis. This is an island in the Delta, nine ropes in circumference. In Prosopitis there are several cities, but that from which the boats go to collect the bones of the bulls is called Atarbechis, and in it there is a holy temple of Aphrodite. From here many men go about the various cities to dig up the bones and bring them back for burial all in one place. And as they do with the horned cattle, so they do with all other cattle that die; for it is against their law to kill these also.

42. All those who worship the Theban Zeus or who live in the district of Thebes sacrifice goats but not sheep. Not all the Egyptians worship the same gods alike, save only Isis and Osiris, who, they say, is Dionysus; these two they all worship alike. Those who have a cult of

the god of Mendes, or who live in the province of that city, sacrifice sheep but not goats. Now the Thebans and those who follow their example in abstaining from sheep give this reason for their custom: they say that Heracles was desirous at all costs of looking upon Zeus, who did not wish to be seen by him. At last, yielding to the importunity of Heracles, Zeus contrived to be seen wearing the head and fleece of a ram which he had beheaded and flayed. Therefore it is that the Egyptians represent Zeus by an image with a ram's head; and they are followed in this by the Ammonians, who are colonists from Egypt and Ethiopia and speak a language made up of words taken from both these nations. And this, I conceive, is the reason why they call themselves Ammonians; for the Egyptians call Zeus Amun. Upon this ground, then, the rain is accounted a sacred animal by the Thebans, and they will not use it for sacrifice. But on one day of the year, the festival of Zeus, they cut a single rain in pieces and flay it and put its fleece over the image of Zeus; then they bring an image of Heracles near to it. Meanwhile all who are present at the ceremony lament for the ram, and afterwards they bury it in a consecrated coffin.

47. Pigs are accounted such unclean beasts by the Egyptians that if a man touch one in passing, he goes to the river and immerses himself with his clothes on him; and swineherds, though by birth Egyptians, are the only men who may not enter any of the temples, nor will any man give his daughter in marriage to one of that calling, nor take a wife from among them; so the swineherds must marry and give in marriage within their own community. The Egyptians think it wrong to sacrifice pigs to any god, save to the moon and to Dionysus when the moon is full; and then they will eat of the flesh. They give a reason for offering pigs at this feast and abhorring them at other sacrifices; but it is not seemly for me to tell what it is, though I know it. But the offering of pigs to the moon is done in this way: when they have killed the victim, they put the end of the tail and the spleen and the caul into the fat that is found about the belly and burn them with funeral rites; and the rest of the flesh they eat at this season of full moon, though at other times they will not taste of it. And poor men, who cannot afford more, make dough into the shape of pigs, and these objects they bake and offer up.

48. On the eve of the feast of Dionysus everyone kills a pig before his door and then restores the carcase to the swineherd who sold the

animal. The rest of this festival they celebrate much as the Greeks do, except for the choral dances; only instead of the phallus they have invented images a cubit high worked by strings, the male organ moving and almost as big as the rest of the body; and these are carried through the villages by women. A flute-player goes before, and the women follow, chanting the praises of Dionysus. Why the male organ is made so big and is the only part of the body made to move is explained by the sacred legend.

49. For my part, I think Melampus, the son of Amytheon, was not ignorant of this ceremony. It was he who introduced the name and the sacrifices of Dionysus among the Greeks and the procession with the phallus. More exactly, he did not teach them the whole rite, but the teachers who followed him did so fully. But Melampus was certainly the first who taught the Greeks to carry the phallus in procession in honour of Dionysus, and it is to him that they owe their knowledge of the rite. I think he was a wise man, skilled in the art of divination, and that he taught the Greeks many things derived from Egypt, especially in the worship of Dionysus, making slight changes in them. For I will not admit that the agreement between the two peoples in the way of honouring this god is the effect of chance: if it were so, the Greek rite would be more Greek in character and older than it is. Nor would I admit that the Egyptians took this or any other of their customs from the Greeks. I believe that Melampus learned the worship of Dionysus chiefly from Cadmus of Tyre and the other Phoenicians who came with Cadmus to the land now called Boeotia.

50. And indeed the names of almost all the gods came to Greece from Egypt. That they came to us from foreign peoples I have found out by enquiry, and I think they came mainly from Egypt. Excepting only Poseidon and the Dioscuri, as I have said, and Hera and Hestia and Themis and the Graces and Nereids, the Egyptians have had the names of all the gods time out of mind. This is what the Egyptians themselves say. Those whose names are unknown in Egypt were, as I think, named by the Pelasgians, excepting Poseidon, of whom knowledge came from the Libyans. For only the Libyans have had the name of this god from the earliest times and have always worshipped him. Nor do the Egyptians pay religious honours to heroes.

51. These observances, then, and others which I shall describe, the Greeks adopted from the Egyptians; but to make images of Hermes

with the male organ erect they learned from the Pelasgians; the
Athenians learned it first and others from their example. For the
Athenians had come to be considered as Greeks by the time that the
Pelasgians came to dwell in their country and thus became a Greek
people likewise. Whoever has been initiated in the mysteries of the
Cabiri, which the people of Samothrace learned from the Pelasgians
and now practise, will know what I mean. For the Pelasgians lived in
Samothrace before they came to Attica, and it is from them that the
rites of this mystery are derived. The Athenians were thus the first of
the Greeks to make these phallic images of Hermes, having learned
from the Pelasgians. And the Pelasgians had a religious fable about it,
which is part of the Samothracian mysteries.

52. In earlier times the Pelasgians called on the gods when they
sacrificed without naming any (this I know, for I was told so at
Dodona), for they had not learned the names.

They called them *gods* because of the belief that all things in the
world were *set* in order and governed by them. After a long time the
Pelasgians received the names of most of the gods from Egypt, and,
much later, that of Dionysus. Thereupon they consulted the oracle at
Dodona concerning the names; for this is accounted the oldest of the
Greek oracles, and at that time it was the only one. When they asked
at Dodona whether they were to receive the names from foreigners, the
oracle answered that they should do so. Thereafter they used the
names of the gods when they sacrificed, and from the Petasgians the
Greeks learned them.

53. But the origin of each god, whether all of them had always
existed and what were their shapes were things that the Greeks knew
not until, I might almost say, the other day. For I suppose that the age
of Hesiod and Homer was not more than four hundred years before my
time; and it was they who introduced the genealogies of the gods
among the Greeks, assigned to them surnames, functions and honours
and clothed them in their several forms. (The earlier part of this is what
the priestesses at Dodona tell: the later, concerning Hesiod and Homer,
is what I myself think.) The poets who are said to have lived before
these two came, as I believe, after them.

54. Concerning the oracles of Greece and Libya the Egyptians have
this to tell. The priests of the Zeus of Thebes told me that two
priestesses were carried away from that country by Phoenicians, who, as

they heard, sold one in Libya and the other in Greece, and these two women established the first oracles in either place. When I asked how they knew this, they said that the Egyptians had searched diligently for these two women, but in vain, and afterwards they had learnt what they now told me.

55. This account I had from the priests at Thebes; but the prophetesses at Dodona say that two black pigeons flew from Thebes of Egypt, one to Libya and the other to Dodona. The second perched on a beech-tree, and uttered human speech admonishing the people of the place to set up an oracle of Zeus; and they, believing it to be a divine revelation, obeyed. They add that the pigeon which flew to Libya commanded the establishment of an oracle of Ammon, also dedicated to Zeus. This is said by the priestesses at Dodona, the oldest of whom is named Promeneia, the next Timarete, and the youngest Nicandra; and the other servants of the shrine said likewise.

56. But my own belief is this. If the Phoenicians did indeed carry off the holy women and sell one in Libya and one in Greece, the part of Greece (called in those days Pelasgia) where they sold the second was Thesprotia. Being kept as a slave there, she consecrated an altar to Zeus under a beech-tree; for we may suppose that she, who had been priestess of his temple at Thebes would be mindful of his worship in another place. Later she made of it a place of divination, when she had learnt the language of Greece; and she must have said that her sister had been sold in Libya by the same Phoenicians.

57. The people of Dodona, I suppose, called these women pigeons because they were foreigners and their speech was no more understood than the chattering of birds; then, when one could speak their language, they reported that the pigeon had spoken with a human voice; for while she spoke a foreign tongue they would think her voice like that of a bird. But how could a pigeon utter the speech of men? And they said the pigeon was black meaning that the woman was an Egyptian.

58. Moreover, it is true that the ways of divination at Thebes of Egypt and at Dodona are much alike; and the foretelling of the future by signs in the victims of the sacrifice began in Egypt.

The Egyptians, too, were the first to hold religious festivals and processions and such solemnities: all these the Greeks learned from them. This I believe because such things among the Egyptians are very ancient, and in Greece they are but lately introduced.

Discussion Question

1. Given your knowledge of Egyptian religious practices and social customs, do you think Herodotus deserves the title of historian?

2. What kinds of parallels does Herodotus draw between Egyptian and Greek customs?

Sources

Herodotus, *The Histories of Herodotus*, trans. Harry Carter, New York: Heritage Press, 1958.

James Romm, *Herodotus*, New Haven and London: Yale University Press, 1998.

PLATO,
APOLOGY OF
SOCRATES

The Greek philosopher Plato first made his mark in Athenian society by
preserving the thoughts of his teacher, Socrates, in a series of dialogues.
In the disillusionment that set in among Athenians after their defeat in the
Peloponnesian War, Socrates was brought to trial for impiety and the
corruption of the city's youth. In the years preceding his execution, he had
cultivated a following among young Athenians like Plato for his methods
of questioning all manner of knowledge. Socrates, reacting against the
moral relativism of the Sophists, advocated an unceasing quest for
absolute truths. He became a colorful but bothersome figure around the
city by questioning the actions of his fellow citizens by way of tightly
constructed dialogues, the so-called Socratic method.

Plato was born around 428 B.C. to distinguished Athenian family.
Rather than follow a career in politics as befitted his status, Plato became
a disciple of Socrates, and after his mentor's death in 399 B.C., traveled
abroad with other disciples to continue his studies. At one point he
participated in a failed attempt to establish an ideal monarchy in Sicily.
When he returned to Athens, he founded the Academy to teach virtue
through the study of philosophy to the youth of his hometown. Although
we know little about how the school functioned, Plato counted among his
students the young Aristotle. Plato turned to questions of politics in his
later writings. Like his first efforts, his work took the form of dialogues.
One of his most famous works, *The Republic,* reveals Plato's cynicism
toward the society that had snuffed out the life of his teacher.

Socrates left no writings, so we know of his philosophy largely
through the writings of Plato. Plato's *Apology of Socrates* reconstructs the
speech that Socrates made in self-defense shortly before his execution. In
this dialogue, Socrates defends himself by arguing that the accusations
leveled at him stem from the maliciousness of those he had dared to

criticize on the streets of Athens. In this particular excerpt, Socrates dissects the charges brought against him, arguing that the bulk of these accusations are nothing more than slander.

APOLOGY OF SOCRATES

Plato

How you, Athenians, have been affected by my accusers, I don't know;
but certainly they made even me almost forget about myself, they were
speaking so persuasively. And yet they have said virtually nothing *true*.
The one I found most surprising among their many falsehoods was this,
when they were saying that you ought to be careful. I don't deceive
you, because I'm a clever speaker. Their failure to be ashamed at the
immediate prospect of my refuting them in practice, when my utter
lack of cleverness in speaking becomes apparent, this struck me as the
very height of their shamelessness—unless after all my opponents give
the title of 'clever speaker' to one who tells the truth; if that's what they
are saying I should agree that I'm an orator in a different league from
them. As I say, then, they have said little or nothing true; but from me
you shall hear nothing but the truth: not, by Zeus, Athenians, language
elegant with fine words and expressions like theirs, or ornate, but you
shall hear speech as it comes and with ordinary words—because I
believe that what I'm saying is just—and none of you should expect
otherwise. It wouldn't indeed be fitting, gentlemen, for a man of my
age to come before you like an adolescent, polishing arguments.
Furthermore, Athenians, I earnestly beg and beseech you: if you hear
me defending myself by means of the same arguments as I normally
use in the Marketplace at the stalls, where many of you have heard me,
and elsewhere too, don't be surprised and don't barrack me because of
this. You see, it's like this: this is the first time I have come to court,
seventy years old though I am. So the language of this place is simply
foreign to me. Therefore, just as if I were really a foreigner you would
no doubt forgive me for speaking in the dialect and manner I was
brought up in, in the present instance I have a just right, I think, to ask
you to pass over my style of speaking—the style may perhaps be
worse or perhaps better—but to consider and pay attention to just this
question, whether what I say is just or not. That indeed is what makes
a good judge; what makes a good orator is truthtelling.

It would be just for me, Athenians, to defend myself first against
the first set of accusations against me, false as they are, and against my

first set of accusers, and after that against the later accusations and accusers. You've heard in fact many people accusing me for a long time, for many years now, and saying nothing true: I'm more afraid of them than of Anytus and his people, even though they too are formidable; more to be feared, gentlemen, are those who took most of you over from your childhood on, and kept both exercising persuasion on you and accusing me, and saying, not in the least truthfully, that there was a certain Socrates, a wise man and investigator of things both above and below the earth, and one who made the weaker argument the stronger. Athenians, the men who spread this rumour are the more formidable of my accusers, since people hearing them think those studying these topics do not even accept gods. What's more, these accusers are numerous, and have been bringing charges against me for a long time now, and in addition they addressed you at an age at which you were specially liable to believe them, being, some of you, boys or adolescents, and their accusations won simply by default in the absence of any defender. What is most unreasonable of all is this, that it is impossible to be certain of and to give their names, unless one of them happens to be a comic playwright. But those who tried to persuade you with malicious slanders, and those who were actually persuaded themselves before trying to persuade other people, these are all very hard to deal with. That's because it's impossible even to bring any of them into court or examine him; one has straightforwardly, as it were, to shadow-box in one's defence and examine with no-one answering the questions. Just as I say, then, you too should conceive my accusers as falling into two sets, one bringing the present accusation, the other being those from long ago that I am talking about; and you should approve my answering the earlier ones first; after all, you heard their accusations before, and also much more than, these later ones'.

Well: it's right, then, to offer a defence, Athenians, and to try to remove from your minds in this short time the slander you took in over a long time. I should like that to happen so, if it's better in any respect both for you and for me, and to achieve something by my defence. But I think it's difficult, and I'm not forgetting the kind of task it is. Nevertheless, let that go how the god pleases; it's right to obey the law and to offer a defence.

So let us take up again from the beginning the question what the accusation is which has given rise to the slanders against me, which indeed Meletus was relying on when he brought in the present indictment. Well: what did the slanderers actually say in their slander? I must read out their affidavit as if they *were* accusers: "Socrates is an offender and a meddler, in studying things below the earth and in the sky, and making the weaker argument into the stronger and instructing other people in these same things." The charge runs something like that. You have seen this picture for yourselves in Aristophanes' comedy, a Socrates being carried round in the play and claiming to walk on air and talking a great deal of other rubbish about subjects on which I'm not an expert at all, not on any point, great or small. And I don't speak by way of insult to such knowledge, if anyone is wise in such matters; I hope I shall not have to defend myself from Meletus on charges as important as that; but really, Athenians, I take no part in these subjects. As witnesses I call most of. you yourselves; I think it right for you to instruct and tell each other, all of you who have ever heard me in discussion—and there are many of you who have—at any rate tell each other whether any of you has ever heard anything great or small from me in discussion about such topics; and you will discover as a result that the rest of what most people say about me is like that too.

But indeed none of these things is so, and certainly not if you have heard from anybody that I try to educate people and charge a fee; that isn't true either. I say this because this too seems to me to be a fine thing, if someone were able to educate people, as Gorgias the Leontine and Prodicus the Cean and Hippias the Eleian do. For each of these, gentlemen, is able to go into any single community and the young men, who may spend time for nothing in the company of any fellow-citizen they wish—they persuade them to leave the company of those people and have theirs, for a fee, and to be grateful besides. I say this because there is another man in Athens from Paros, a wise man I realised was in town; indeed I happened to approach a man who has paid more money to sophists than everyone else put together, Callias son of Hipponicus. Anyway I asked him—since he has two sons: "Callias", I said, "if your two sons had been a pair of colts or calves we should have been able to put someone in charge of them and hire a man likely to make them fine and good in the appropriate goodness, and this man would have been either an equestrian or an agriculturalist. But as things are, since they are a pair of human beings, who do you have it in mind to put in charge of them? Who is there who is expert in the appropriate goodness, both that of a human being and that of a citizen? I ask because I imagine you have investigated this on account of your possessing sons. Is there any such man," I said, "or not?" "Very much so," he said. "Who", I said, "and where from, and at what price does he teach?" "Evenus, Socrates," he said, "from Paros, for five minae." And I congratulated Evenus if he truly possessed this skill, and teaches it so reasonably. I at least for my part would actually be priding myself and putting on airs if I knew these things; but indeed I don't know them, Athenians.

At this point one of you might perhaps answer: "But, Socrates. what *is* your activity? Where have these slanderous reports about you come from? It's not the case, surely, that, without your pursuing any activity more unusual than other men, nevertheless such rumour and talk have started, if you weren't active in any way differently from most men. So tell us what it is, so that we don't improvise stories about you." These remarks strike me as just remarks to make, and I will try to explain to you what it can be which has given rise to both my reputation and the slander. Now listen: I shall perhaps strike some of you as joking; but you should know that I shall be telling you nothing but the truth. I have, Athenians, acquired this reputation on account of nothing other than a sort of wisdom. What kind of wisdom is that? The very one which is perhaps human; in truth I probably am indeed wise in that. But perhaps the other men I just mentioned are wise in some superhuman wisdom—or else I don't know what to say; certainly I am not an expert in it, and the man who says I am is uttering a falsehood and speaking slander to my detriment. Now please, Athenians, don't barrack me, even if I strike you as boasting. What I'm going to say is not my own saying, and I will refer you to its original source, one you can trust. About my—whether indeed I have any wisdom, and what sort it is, I shall call as witness before you the god of Delphi: you know, I suppose, about Chaerephon—he was a friend of mine from my youth, and not only was a friend to your democracy, but also accompanied you into that exile of yours, and came back from exile with you—you know, anyway, what sort of person Chaerephon was, how eager in pursuit of his goals. In particular, he once went to Delphi and ventured to consult the Oracle on this point—now, as I said, don't barrack, gentlemen—he asked whether anyone was wiser than me.

Well, the Pythian priestess responded that no-one was wiser. And to this his brother here will witness, since Chaerephon is dead.

Consider my reasons for saying this: I'm about to tell you where the slander about me has come from. Now when I heard the story my thoughts ran like this: 'What on earth is the god saying, and what on earth lies behind his riddle? In nothing, great or small, do I know that I am wise. What on earth, then, is he saying when he claims that I am the wisest? He *can't* be speaking falsely; that's not permissible for him.' And to begin with for a long time I was in doubt about what on earth he was saying. Then, with great difficulty I made up my mind to inquire into it in some such way as this: I went to see one of those who appear to be wise, on the grounds that there, if indeed anywhere, I should refute the prophecy and show the Oracle, "This man here is wiser than me, but you said I was." In examining this man, then,— there's no need for me to name him, but it was a politician I was investigating when I had this sort of experience, Athenians—and in my discussion with him this man struck me as being thought to be wise by many other people and especially by himself, but not as being wise. And then I tried to show him that, though he thought he was wise, he wasn't. So, as a result of this, he and many of the people who were there took a dislike to me; but I thought to myself as I went off that I was wiser than this person at least: probably indeed neither of us knew anything fine and good, but he thought he knew something he didn't know, whereas I, just as I didn't know, didn't think I knew. I *seemed* likely therefore to be wiser than him by virtue of a small thing, this very point, that what I didn't know I didn't think I knew either. From there I went on to another of those thought to be rather wise, and arrived at the very same opinion and then he too and many others took a dislike to me.

Next, by now I was going on in order, with the perception (in grief and fear) that people disliked me, but with the apparent necessity nevertheless of setting the greatest store by the matter of the god—so had to go on, in considering the question what the Oracle was saying, to everyone who was thought to know something. And, by the Dog Athenians—to tell you the truth, as I must—I swear something like this happened to me: those with the highest reputation struck me almost as the ones most deficient, as I made inquiries in relation to the god, and others, thought to be less significant, as being abler with respect to good sense. I ought to explain to you these wanderings of mine, like those of a man undertaking something like labours, to find the oracle unrefuted. After the politicians I went on to the poets, both the composers of tragedies and those of dithyrambs, and the rest, thinking that there I would catch myself in the act of being more ignorant than them. So, taking up again those poems of theirs which struck me as especially thoroughly crafted, I would ask them what they were saying, with the object also at the same time of learning something from them. I blush therefore, to tell you, gentlemen, the truth of the matter; but nevertheless I am obliged to tell you. Virtually almost all the bystanders would have spoken better than them on the subjects on which they themselves had written. So I became aware also in the case of the poets too, quickly, that they did not compose their compositions by wisdom, but by some sort of natural gift, and under divine possession just like the prophets and composers of oracles—since these too say many fine things, but know nothing of what they say. Something like that seemed to me to have happened to the poets too, and at the same time I noticed that they thought by reason of their poetic craft that they were the wisest of men in other subjects too, in subjects where they were not. So I passed on from them too, thinking that I had excelled them in the very same respect as I had the politicians also.

Finally, then, I came to the handcraftsmen; this, because I was conscious of knowing, myself, almost nothing, but I knew that I should find at least them knowing many fine things. And in this I was not mistaken, and they knew things I did not know, and in that respect they were wiser than me. But, Athenians, they struck me, the good workmen too, as making just the same error as the poets: because of their fine mastery in their arts, each claimed to be very wise in other— and the most important—matters too; and this inconcinnity of theirs covered up their actual wisdom; the result was that I asked myself on the Oracle's behalf whether I would accept my being just the way I am, in no respect wise in their kind of wisdom, nor ignorant with their ignorance, or my having both their qualities. The answer I gave myself and the Oracle was that I was better off just the way I am.

As a result of this inquiry, Athenians, I have acquired widespread dislike, and of the most troublesome and unpleasant kind. The dislike has given rise to many slanders, and to my being described by this word, as "wise". This is because, each time, the bystanders think that I am myself wise in subjects in which I refute someone else. But the probability is, gentlemen, that in truth the god is wise, and that in that oracle he is saying this, that human wisdom is worth little or nothing. He seems, moreover, to be talking about this Socrates, and to be using my name in addition, by way of constituting me an example, as if he were to say: "That one of you, mortal men, is wisest who, just like Socrates, has realised that in truth he is worth nothing in respect of wisdom." These, then, as I go about, are the inquiries and explorations I am still even now, as I go around, putting in accordance with the god to any fellow-townsman or foreigner that I think wise. And when he does not strike me thus, I come to the god's aid and demonstrate that he is not wise. And it is because of this occupation that I have had no leisure to pursue any of the state's affairs to speak of, or my family affairs, but am in deep poverty on account of my service of the god.

What is more, the young men who follow me around, those with the most spare time, the sons of the wealthiest fathers, of their own accord—these take pleasure in listening to people being examined, and often themselves copy me, and try accordingly to examine other people; and then, I suppose, they find a great abundance of people who think they know something, but know little or nothing. The result is, then, that those examined by them are angry with me, not with themselves, and say that a certain Socrates is a great villain and corrupts the young men. And whenever they are asked by what action and by what instruction, they have nothing to say and are ignorant, but to avoid being thought to be in a difficulty they use the answers that lie ready to hand against all philosophers: "the heavens and the world below the earth" and "not accepting the gods" and "making the weaker argument into the stronger"; the truth, I think, they would refuse to tell, that they become conspicuous for claiming knowlege but knowing nothing. Being therefore, I imagine, eager for respect, and emotional, and numerous, and speaking about me vigorously and persuasively, they have filled your ears with long-standing and emotional slanders. For these reasons Meletus has attacked me, and Anytus and Lycon, Meletus in annoyance on the poets' behalf, Anytus on the craftsmen's and the politicians', and Lycon on the orators'. In consequence, just as I said at the beginning, I should be surprised if I were able to remove this slander from your minds in so short a time when there has been so much of it. Here you have, Athenians, the truth, and I speak without hiding from you anything I great or small, and without keeping anything back. And in fact I virtually know that these very people dislike me, which is actual evidence that I'm speaking the truth, and that this is the slander against me, and these are the reasons. And whether you inquire into all this now or on another occasion, you will find it to be so.

Now on the accusations my first accusers used to bring against me that must be a sufficient defence before you. But against Meletus—that good and patriotic man, as he says—and the later ones I shall try to defend myself next. Once more, as if they were a different set of accusers, let us take, again, *their* affidavit. It runs something like this: he says Socrates is an offender in that he corrupts the young men and does not accept the gods the city accepts, but other novel superhuman beings. The charge is of that sort; but let us examine each single point of this charge.

Discussion Questions

1. What crimes was Socrates accused of? How does Plato, using the voice of Socrates, explain and justify those actions?

2. How does Socrates construct his argument? What kinds of strategies or rhetorical devices does he employ to make his defense more convincing?

Sources

Plato, *Apology of Socrates*, trans. Michael C. Stokes, Warminster: Aris & Phillips Ltd., 1997.

R.B. Rutherford, *The Art of Plato: Ten Essays in Platonic Interpretation*, Cambridge, MA: Harvard University Press, 1995.

CHAPTER 3

Arrian

The Life of Alexander the Great

ARRIAN, *THE LIFE OF ALEXANDER THE GREAT*

Arrian of Nicomedia transcended the barriers between the Greek and Roman worlds by making a career serving the Roman empire while retaining his affinity for and appreciation of Greek traditions. Born around 89 A.D. in the city of Nicomedia, a crossroads of commercial and military traffic along a northern Asia Minor trade route, Arrian belonged to a family of the local aristocracy. For reasons of political and economic expediency, his family had been granted Roman citizenship some generations earlier with the annexation of Bithynia into the Roman empire, yet they remained Greek in their cultural orientation.

In his late teens, Arrian traveled to the Greek town of Nicopolis to study with the Stoic philosopher Epictetus, on whom he would later write several books, establishing himself as a philosopher. However, Arrian chose to pursue a career in military and governmental service. Arrian served the Roman empire as proconsul, consul, and imperial legate. His successes were aided by the patronage of several high-ranking Roman officials, as well as from his own talents and resources. He also shared the emperor Hadrian's passion for hunting, which likely furthered his ascent to the legateship. At the end of his life, Arrian settled in Athens, choosing a cultural hub rather than a center of political and military power or a quiet retirement in Nicomedia. He became an Athenian citizen and held the office of archon, a rare honor for a non-Athenian.

Aside from his books on Epictetus, Arrian wrote on hunting, military strategy, and most notably, history. He preferred the Greek tradition of local history rather than focusing on his experiences in Rome, as was customary for most senators. Among his works we find a history of Bithynia before its annexation by Rome, a chronicle of Roman-Parthian relations, and another work recounting the opposition of Parthia to Roman rule. Yet his most famous historical work was devoted the exploits of

Alexander the Great. Arrian attempted to portray the military genius and noble character of Alexander, challenging several of the Macedonian ruler's detractors in the process. In the passage below, Arrian describes the passage of Alexander and his troops to India and Persia, where several anecdotes illustrate how Alexander managed to assimilate such diverse groups of people into his empire.

THE LIFE OF ALEXANDER THE GREAT

By Arrian

BOOK SEVEN

On reaching Pasargadae and Persepolis, Alexander had a sudden impulse to sail down the Euphrates and Tigris into the Persian Gulf; he had already seen something of the mouths of the Indus and of the waters beyond them, and now he wished to do the same with the Tigris and Euphrates. We find in some writers the statement that he intended to sail right round Arabia, Ethiopia, and Libya, pressing forward past the Nomads beyond Mount Atlas to Gadeira, and so into the Mediterranean; thus, had he added Libya and Carthage to his conquests, he could with full justification have claimed the title of King of All Asia, unlike the Median and Persian kings, who, ruling as they did only a fraction of that continent, could not properly call themselves Great Kings at dl. Some authorities say that he proposed subsequently to sail into the Black Sea and on to Scythian territory by the Sea of Azov; others, that he meant to make for Sicily and southern Italy to check the Romans, whose reputation, being greatly on the increase, was already causing him concern.

Personally I have no data from which to infer precisely what Alexander had in mind, and I do not care to make guesses; one thing, however, I feel I can say without fear of contradiction, and that is that his plans, whatever they were, had no lack of grandeur or ambition: he would never have remained idle in the enjoyment of any of his conquests, even had he extended his empire from Asia to Europe and from Europe to the British Isles. On the contrary, he would have continued to seek beyond them for unknown lands, as it was ever his nature, if he had no rival, to strive to better his own best.

I have always liked tile story of the Indian sages, some of whom Alexander chanced to come upon out of doors in a meadow, where they used to meet to discuss philosophy. On the appearance of Alexander and his army, these venerable men stamped with their feet and gave no other sign of interest. Alexander asked them through interpreters what they meant by this odd behaviour, and they replied:

'King Alexander, every man can possess only so much of the earth's surface as this we are standing on. You are but human like the rest of us, save that you are always busy and up to no good, travelling so many miles from your home, a nuisance to yourself and to others. Ah well! You will soon be dead, and then you will own just as much of this earth as will suffice to bury you.' Alexander expressed his approval of these sage words; but in point of fact his conduct was always the exact opposite of what he then professed to admire. On another occasion he is said to have expressed surprise at a remark made by Diogenes of Sinope: he was marching somewhere in the Isthmus with a contingent of Longshields and footguards, and chancing to see Diogenes lying in the sun, he stopped and asked him if there was anything he wanted.

'Nothing,' replied the philosopher; 'though I should be grateful if you and your friends would move to one side, and not keep the sun off me.'

One must admit, then, that Alexander was not wholly a stranger to the loftier flights of philosophy; but the fact remains that he was, to an extraordinary degree, the slave of ambition. In Taxila, once, he met some members of the Indian sect of Wise Men whose practice it is to go naked, and he so much admired their powers of endurance that the fancy took him to have one of them in his personal train. The oldest man among them, whose name was Dandamis (the others were his pupils), refused either to join Alexander himself or to permit any of his pupils to do so. 'If you, my lord,' he is said to have replied, are the son of God, why—so am I. I want nothing from you, for what I have suffices. I perceive, moreover, that the men you lead get no good from their world-wide wandering over land and sea, and that of their many journeyings there will be no end. I desire nothing that you can give me; I fear no exclusion from any blessings which may perhaps be yours. India, with the fruits of her soil in due season is enough for me while I live; and when I die, I shall be rid of my poor body—my unseemly housemate.' These words convinced Alexander that Dandamis was, in a true sense, a free man; so he made no attempt to compel him. On the other hand, another of these Indian teachers, a man named Calanus, did yield to Alexander's persuasion; this man, according to Megasthenes' account, was declared by his fellow teachers to be a slave to fleshly lusts, an accusation due, no doubt, to the fact that he chose to renounce the bliss of their own asceticism and to serve another master instead of God.

I have mentioned this because no history of Alexander would be complete without the story of Calanus. In India Calanus had never been ill, but when he was living in Persia all strength ultimately left his body. In spite of his enfeebled state he refused to submit to an invalid regimen, and told Alexander that he was content to die as he was, which would be preferable to enduring the misery of being forced to alter his way of life. Alexander, at some length, tried to talk him out of his obstinacy, but to no purpose; then, convinced that if he were any further opposed he would find one means or another of making away with himself, he yielded to his request, and gave instructions for the building of a funeral pyre under the supervision of Ptolemy son of Lagus, of the Personal Guard. Some say Calanus was escorted to the pyre by a solemn procession—horses men, soldiers in armour, and people carrying all kinds of precious oils and spices to throw upon the flames; other accounts mention drinking-cups of silver and gold and kingly robes. He was too ill to walk, and a horse was provided for him; but he was incapable of mounting it, and had to be carried on a litter, upon which he lay with his head wreathed with garlands in the Indian fashion, and singing Indian songs, which his countrymen declare were hymns of praise to their gods. The horse he was to have ridden was of the royal breed of Nysa, and before he mounted the pyre he gave it to Lysimachus, one of his pupils in philosophy, and distributed among other pupils and friends the drinking-cups and draperies which Alexander had ordered to be burnt in his honour upon the pyre.

At last he mounted the pyre and with due ceremony laid himself down. All the troops were watching. Alexander could not but feel that there was a sort of indelicacy in witnessing such a spectacle—the man, after all, had been his friend; everyone else, however, felt nothing but astonishment to see Calanus give not the smallest sign of shrinking from the flames. We read in Nearchus' account of this incident that at the moment the fire was kindled there was, by Alexander's orders, an impressive salute: the bugles sounded, the troops with one accord roared out their battle-cry, and the elephants joined in with their shrill war-trumpetings.

This story and others to a similar effect have been recorded by good authorities; they are not without value to anyone who cares for evidence of the unconquerable resolution of the human spirit in carrying a chosen course of action through to the end.

About this time Alexander sent out Atropates to his province. He had himself gone on to Susa, where he had Abulites arrested and put to death for abusing his office as governor. Abulites' son Oxathres shared the same fate. In the various countries subdued by Alexander there had been a great many irregularities on the part of government officials, acts of violence against individuals, and robbing of temples and tombs. The reason is not far to seek, for Alexander had been away for a very long time in India, and nobody really felt he was ever likely to return from the innumerable hostile nations of the East—not to mention the elephants!—but would find a grave somewhere beyond the Indus, Hydaspes, Acesines, and Hyphasis. Again, the disasters in the Gedrosian desert were a further encouragement to the governors of these more westerly parts to shrug off the idea of his ever, getting safely home. None the less, it must be admitted that, by all accounts, Alexander at this period had become readier to accept as wholly reliable the charges which were made to him against officials, and to inflict severe punishment even for minor offences, in the belief that the sort of attitude which allowed an official to commit some petty irregularity might also lead him to serious crime.

Here at Susa he held wedding ceremonies for the high officers of the Hetaeri; he also took a wife himself—Barsine, Darius' eldest daughter, and, according to Aristobulus, another as well, namely Parysatis, the youngest daughter of Ochus. He had already married Roxane, daughter of Oxyartes of Bactria. To Hephaestion he gave Drypetis, another of Darius' daughters and sister of his own wife Barsine, as he wanted to be uncle to Hephaestion's children; to Craterus he gave Amastrine, daughter of Darius' brother Oxyartes, and to Perdiccas a daughter of Atropates, governor of Media. The bride of Ptolemy (of the Guard) was Artacama, daughter of Artabazus, and Eumenes, the King's secretary, had her sister Artonis; Nearchus was given the daughter of Barsine, and Mentor, Seleucus, the daughter of Spita.menes of Bactria. Similarly, the other officers—to the number of eighty all told—were given as brides young women of the noblest Persian and Median blood. The marriage ceremonies were in the Persian fashion: chairs were set for the bridegrooms in order of precedence, and when healths had been drunk the brides entered and sat down by their bridegrooms, who took them by the hand and kissed them. The King, who was married just as the others were, and in the same place, was the first to perform the ceremony—Alexander was always capable of putting himself on a footing of equality and comradeship with his subordinates, and everyone felt that this act of his was the best proof of his ability to do so. After the ceremony all the men took their wives home, and for every one of them Alexander provided a dowry. There proved to be over 10,000 other Macedonians who had married Asian women; Alexander had them all registered, and every man of them received a wedding gift.

This also seemed a fitting occasion to clear off the men's debts, and Alexander ordered a detailed schedule to be prepared, with a promise of settlement. At first only a few entered their names, suspecting that the order might be a scheme of Alexander's for detecting the spendthrifts who had failed to make do with their army pay. Alexander was annoyed when he learned that most of the men were refusing to enter their names and concealing their possession of covenants to pay, and told them in no uncertain terms what he thought of their suspicions; a King, he declared, is in duty bound to speak nothing but the truth to his subjects, who, in their turn, have no right to suppose that he ever does otherwise. He had tables set up in the army quarters, with money on them, and instructed the clerks in charge to pay off the debts of every man who produced an I.O.U. without even registering their names. After that the troops could not but believe in Alexander's good faith, and they were even more grateful for the concealment of their names than for having their debts payed. This gift to his men is said to have amounted to 20,000 talents—over £4,000,000.

He also made a number of other money awards for distinguished conduct in the field, or in recognition of a man's reputation for good service generally. A special decoration consisting of a gold crown was granted to certain officers for conspicuous bravery: the recipients were Peucestas—for saving the King's life; Leonnatus—also for saving the King's life, for hard service in India, for his victory in Oria, for facing and defeating in battle, with the forces left under his command, the rebellious Oreitae and their neighbours, and his satisfactory settlement of affairs in general in Oria; Nearchus (now also arrived at Susa) for his voyage from India along the coasts of the Indian ocean; Onesicritus, master of the royal galley; and, finally, Hephaestion and the other members of the Personal Guard.

Here in Susa, Alexander received the various officials in charge of affairs in the newly built towns and the governors of the territories he had previously overrun. They brought with them some 30,000 young fellows, all boys of the same age, all wearing the Macedonian battledress and trained on Macedonian lines. Alexander called them his *Epigoni*—'inheritors'—and it is said that their coming caused much bad feeling among the Macedonians, who felt it was an indication of his many efforts to lessen his dependence for the future upon his own countrymen. Already the sight of Alexander in Median clothes had caused them no little distress, and most of them had found the Persian marriage ceremonies by no means to their taste—even some of the actual participants had objected to the foreign form of the ceremony, in spite of the fact that they were highly honoured by being, for the occasion, on a footing of equality with the King. They resented, too, the growing orientalism of Peucestas, Governor of Persia, who, to Alexander's evident satisfaction, had adopted the Persian language and dress, just as they resented the inclusion of foreign mounted troops in the regiments of the Hetaeri: Bactrians, Sogdians, Arachotians; Zarangians, Areians, Parthians, and the so-called Euacae from Persia were all introduced into the crack Macedonian cavalry regiments, provided they had some outstanding personal recommendation, such as good looks, or whatever it might be. Besides this, a fifth mounted regiment was formed; it did not consist entirely of oriental troops, but formed an addition to the total cavalry strength and had a certain number of foreign troops posted to it. Foreign officers were also posted to the Guard—Cophen son of Artabazus, Hydarnes and Artiboles sons of Mazaeus, Sisines and Phradasmenes sons of Phrataphernes, the satrap of Parthia and Hyrcania, Histanes son of Oxyartes and brother of Alexander's wife Roxane, Autobares and his brother Mithrobaeus. The command was given to Hystaspes, a Bactrian, and the orientals were all equipped with the Macedonian spear in place of their native javelin. All this was a cause of deep resentment to the Macedonians, who could not but feel that Alexander's whole outlook was becoming tainted with orientalism, and that he no longer cared a rap for his own people or his own native ways. groups of people into his empire.

Discussion Questions

1. How did Alexander, according to Arrian, treat conquered peoples? How effective were his strategies?

2. What kind of an impression of Alexander's character does Arrian try to convey? Do you find this impression convincing?

Sources

Arrian, *The Life of Alexander the Great*, trans. Aubrey de Sélincourt, Great Britain: Penguin, 1958.

Philip A. Stadter, *Arrian of Nicomedia*, Chapel Hill: University of North Carolina Press, 1980.

CHAPTER 4

Virgil

Aeneid

Strabo

The Geography of Strabo

VIRGIL, *AENEID*

Virgil, the Roman poet, was born in 70 B.C. near Mantua in Cisalpine
Gaul. This region had once been hellenized, but fell under the rule of
Rome sometime in the second century B.C. His father, a farmer, sent him
to be educated first in Cremona, and later to Rome. He then spent a
decade farming the family land and writing poetry about the beauty of his
rural surroundings until the ruling triumvirate confiscated the family farm
in order to grant the land to demobilized soldiers in 41 B.C. Virgil returned
to Rome, where he was accepted into the circle of poets supported by
Augustus, and his advisor Maecenas. His first major works idealized the
countryside and pastoral life. He received praise for his first publication,
the Eclogues, a series of pastoral poems. Virgil left Rome to study
Epicurean philosophy in a community of scholars located around Naples,
where his generous patrons permitted him to keep a villa. His next
publication, the *Georgics,* again focused on rural themes and established
his reputation as one of the finest poets of his time.

After his famous renunciation in 27 B.C., Augustus ruled over the
Roman empire virtually unchallenged. The political fortunes of Augustus
prompted Virgil, perhaps with the emperor's encouragement, to undertake
an epic work that would immortalize the emperor and the honor of Rome.
Virgil devoted the remaining decade of his life to composing this poem.
The main character, Aeneas, founds the city of Rome during his
wanderings. Virgil modeled the *Aeneid* after Homer's epics, but Aeneas
never falls prey to the human weaknesses of Achilles or Ulysses, the
heroes of the *Iliad* and the *Odyssey.* Instead, his resolve results in glory
for the Roman state, mirroring Augustus' efforts to expand the empire.
The poem further glorified the emperor by implying that Augustus had
descended from the hero of the poem.

In the *Aeneid,* Aeneas journeys to Carthage before founding Rome. There he meets Dido, the founder and queen of that great city. The story of their love affair and its tragic outcome demonstrate Virgil's talents as both poet and storyteller. In the verses below, Mercury approaches Aeneas to command him to leave Dido for the Italian peninsula. The gods have deemed that Aeneas cannot remain in Carthage and leave his destiny unfulfilled. Aeneas obeys unquestioningly, but Dido is heartbroken, and resolves to die.

AENEID

Virgil

As soon as his winged feet have touched the outskirts,
he sees Aeneas founding fortresses
and fashioning new houses. And his sword
was starred with tawny jasper, and the cloak
that draped his shoulders blazed with Tyrian purple-   350
a gift that wealthy Dido wove for him;
she had run golden thread along the web.
And Mercury attacks at once. "Are you
now laying the foundation of high Carthage,
as servant to a woman, building her   355
a splendid city here? Are you forgetful
of what is your own kingdom, your own fate?
The very god of gods, whose power sways
both earth and heaven, sends me down to you
from bright Olympus. He himself has asked me   360
to carry these commands through the swift air:
what are you pondering or hoping for
while squandering your ease in Libyan lands?
For if the brightness of such deeds is not
enough to kindle you—if you cannot   365
attempt the task for your own fame—remember
Ascanius growing up, the hopes you hold
for Iülus, your own heir, to whom are owed
the realm of Italy and land of Rome."
So did Gyllene's god speak out. He left   370
the sight of mortals even as he spoke
and vanished into the transparent air.

This vision stunned Aeneas, struck him dumb;
his terror held his hair erect; his voice
held fast within his jaws. He burns to flee   375
from Carthage; he would quit these pleasant lands,
astonished by such warnings, the command
of gods. What can he do? With what words dare

he face the frenzied queen? What openings
can he employ? His wits are split, they shift 380
here, there; they race to different places, turning
to everything. But as he hesitated,
this seemed the better plan: he calls Sergestus
and Mnestheus and the strong Serestus, and
he asks them to equip the fleet in silence, 385
to muster their companions on the shore,
to ready all their arms, but to conceal
the reasons for this change; while he himself—
with gracious Dido still aware of nothing
and never dreaming such a love could ever 390
be broken—would try out approaches, seek
the tenderest, most tactful time for speech,
whatever dexterous way might suit his case.
And all are glad. They race to carry out
the orders of Aeneas, his commands. 395

But Dido—for who can deceive a lover?—
had caught his craftiness; she quickly sensed
what was to come; however safe they seemed,
she feared all things. That same unholy Rumor
brought her these hectic tidings: that the boats 400
were being armed, made fit for voyaging.
Her mind is helpless; raging frantically,
inflamed, she raves throughout the city—just
as a Bacchante when, each second year,
she is startled by the shaking of the sacred 405
emblems, the orgies urge her on, the cry
"o Bacchus" calls to her by night; Cithaeron
incites her with its clamor. And at last
Dido attacks Aeneas with these words:

"Deceiver, did you even hope to hide 410
so harsh a crime, to leave this land of mine
without a word? Can nothing hold you back—
neither your love, the hand you pledged, nor even
the cruel death that lies in wait for Dido?

Beneath the winter sky are you preparing   415
a fleet to rush away across the deep
among the north winds, you who have no feeling?
What! Even if you were not seeking out
strange fields and unknown dwellings, even if
your ancient Troy were still erect, would you   420
return to Troy across such stormy seas?
Do you flee me? By tears, by your right hand—
this sorry self is left with nothing else—
by wedding, by the marriage we began,
if I did anything deserving of you   425
or anything of mine was sweet to you,
take pity on a fallen house, put off
your plan, I pray—if there is still place for prayers.
Because of you the tribes of Libya, all
the Nomad princes hate me, even my   430
own Tyrians are hostile; and for you
my honor is gone and that good name that once
was mine, my only claim to reach the stars.
My guest, to whom do you consign this dying
woman? I must say 'guest': this name is all   435
I have of one whom once I called my husband,
Then why do I live on? Until Pygmalion,
my brother, batters down my walls, until
Iarbas the Gaetulian takes me prisoner?
Had I at least before you left conceived   440
a son in me; if there were but a tiny
Aeneas playing by me in the hall,
whose face, in spite of everything, might yet
remind me of you, then indeed I should
not seem so totally abandoned, beaten."   445

Her words were ended. But Aeneas, warned
by Jove, held still his eyes; he struggled, pressed
care back within his breast. With halting words
he answers her at last: "I never shall
deny what you deserve, the kindnesses   450
that you could tell; I never shall regret

remembering Elissa for as long
as I remember my own self, as long
as breath is king over these limbs. I'll speak
brief words that fit the case. I never hoped   455
to hide—do not imagine that—my flight;
I am not furtive. I have never held
the wedding torches as a husband; I
have never entered into such agreements.
If fate had granted me to guide my life   460
by my own auspices and to unravel
my troubles with unhampered will, then I
should cherish first the town of Troy, the sweet
remains of my own people and the tall
rooftops of Priam would remain, my hand   465
would plant again a second Pergamus
for my defeated men. But now Grynean
Apollo's oracles would have me seize
great Italy, the Lycian prophecies
tell me of Italy: there is my love,   470
there is my homeland. If the fortresses
of Carthage and the vision of a city
in Libya can hold you, who are Phoenician,
why, then, begrudge the Trojans' settling on
Ausonian soil? There is no harm: it is   475
right that we, too, seek out a foreign kingdom.

For often as the night conceals the earth
with dew and shadows, often as the stars
ascend, afire, my father's anxious image
approaches me in dreams. Anchises warns   480
and terrifies; I see the wrong I have done
to one so dear, my boy Ascanius,
whom I am cheating of Hesperia,
the fields assigned by fate. And now the gods'
own messenger, sent down by Jove himself—   485
I call as witness both our lives—has brought
his orders through the swift air. My own eyes
have seen the god as he was entering

our walls—in broad daylight. My ears have drunk
his words. No longer set yourself and me   490
afire. Stop your quarrel. It is not
my own free wilt that leads to Italy."

But all the while Aeneas spoke, she stared
askance at him, her glance ran this way, that.
She scans his body with her silent eyes.   495
Then Dido thus, inflamed, denounces him:

"No goddess was your mother, false Aeneas,
and Dardanus no author of your race;
the bristling Caucasus was father to you
on his harsh crags; Hyrcanian tigresses   500
gave you their teats. And why must I dissemble?
Why hold myself in check? For greater wrongs?
For did Aeneas groan when I was weeping?
Did he once turn his eyes or, overcome,
shed tears or pity me, who was his loved one?   505
What shall I cry out first? And what shall follow?
No longer now does mighty Juno or
our Father, son of Saturn, watch this earth
with righteous eyes. Nowhere is certain trust.
He was an outcast on the shore, in want.   510
I took him in and madly let him share
my kingdom; his lost fleet and his companions
I saved from death. Oh I am whirled along
in fire by the Furies! First the augur
Apollo, then the Lycian oracles,   515
and now, sent down by Jove himself, the gods'
own herald, carrying his horrid orders.
This seems indeed to be a work for High Ones,
a care that can disturb their calm. I do not
refute your words. I do not keep you back.   520
Go then, before the winds, to Italy.
Seek out your kingdom overseas; indeed,
if there be pious powers still, I hope
that you will drink your torments to the lees

among sea rocks and, drowning, often cry   525
the name of Dido. Then, though absent, I
shall hunt you down with blackened firebrands;
and when chill death divides my soul and body,
a Shade, I shall be present everywhere.
Depraved, you then will pay your penalties.   530
And I shall hear of it, and that report
will come to me below, among the Shadows."

Her speech is broken off; heartsick, she shuns
the light of day, deserts his eyes; she turns
away, leaves him in fear and hesitation,   535
Aeneas longing still to say so much.
As Dido faints, her servants lift her up;
they carry her into her marble chamber;
they lay her body down upon the couch.

But though he longs to soften, soothe her sorrow   540
and turn aside her troubles with sweet words,
though groaning long and shaken in his mind
because of his great love, nevertheless
pious Aeneas carries out the gods'
instructions. Now he turns back to his fleet.   545

At this the Teucrians indeed fall to.
They launch their tall ships all along the beach;
they set their keels, well-smeared with pitch, afloat.
The crewmen, keen for flight, haul from the forest
boughs not yet stripped of leaves to serve as oars   550
and timbers still untrimmed. And one could see them
as, streaming, they rushed down from all the city:
even as ants, remembering the winter,
when they attack a giant stack of spelt
to store it in their homes; the black file swarms   555
across the fields; they haul their plunder through
the grass on narrow tracks; some strain against
the great grains with their shoulders, heaving hard;
some keep the columns orderly and chide
the loiterers; the whole trail boils with work.   560

What were your feelings, Dido, then? What were
the sighs you uttered at that sight, when far
and wide, from your high citadel, you saw
the beaches boil and turmoil take the waters,
with such a vast uproar before your eyes?   565
Voracious Love, to what do you not drive
the hearts of men? Again, she must outcry,
again, a suppliant, must plead with him,
must bend her pride to love—and so not die
in vain, and with some way still left untried.   570

"Anna, you see them swarm across the beaches;
from every reach around they rush to sea:
the canvas calls the breezes, and already
the boisterous crewmen crown the sterns with garlands.
But I was able to foresee this sorrow;   575
therefore I can endure it, sister; yet
in wretchedness I must ask you for this
one service, Anna. Treacherous Aeneas
has honored you alone, confiding even
his secret feelings unto you; and you   580
alone know all his soft approaches, moods.
My sister, go—to plead with him, to carry
this message to my arrogant enemy.
I never trafficked with the Creeks at Aulis
to root the Trojans out, I never sent   585
a fleet to Pergamus, never disturbed
his father's ashes or Anchises' Shade,
that now Aeneas should ward off my words
from his hard ears. Where is he hurrying?
If he would only grant his wretched lover   590
this final gift: to wait for easy sailing
and favoring winds. I now no longer ask
for those old ties of marriage he betrayed,
nor that he lose his kingdom, be deprived
of lovely Latium; I only ask   595
for empty time, a rest and truce for all
this frenzy, until fortune teaches me,

defeated,how to sorrow. I ask this—
pity your sister—as afinal kindness.
When he has granted it, I shall repay   600
my debt, and with full interest, by my death."

So Dido pleads, and her poor sister carries
these lamentations, and she brings them back.
For lamentation cannot move Aeneas;
his graciousness toward any plea is gone.   605
Fate is opposed, the god makes deaf the hero's
kind ears. As when, among the Alps, north winds
will strain against each other to root out
with blasts—now on this side, now that—a stout
oak tree whose wood is full of years; the roar   610
is shattering, the trunk is shaken, and
high branches scatter on the ground; but it
still grips the rocks; as steeply as it thrusts
its crown into the upper air, so deep
the roots it reaches down to Tartarus: 615
no less than this, the hero; he is battered
on this side and on that by assiduous words;
he feels care in his mighty chest, and yet
his mind cannot be moved; the tears fall, useless.

Then maddened by the fates, unhappy Dido   620
calls out at last for death; it tires her
to see the curve of heaven. That she may
not weaken in her plan to leave the light,
she sees, while placing offerings on the altars
with burning incense-terrible to tell—   625
the consecrated liquid turning black,
the outpoured wine becoming obscene blood.
But no one learns of this, not even Anna.
And more: inside her palace she had built
a marble temple to her former husband   630
that she held dear and honored wonderfully.
She wreathed that shrine with snow-white fleeces and
holy-day leaves. And when the world was seized

by night, she seemed to hear the voice and words
of her dead husband, calling out to Dido.   635
Alone above the housetops, death its song,
an owl often complains and draws its long
slow call into a wailing lamentation.

More, many prophecies of ancient seers
now terrify her with their awful warnings.   640
And in her dreams it is the fierce Aeneas
himself who drives her to insanity;
she always finds herself alone, abandoned,
and wandering without companions on
an endless journey, seeking out her people,   645
her Tyrians in a deserted land:
even as Pentheus, when he is seized by frenzy,
sees files of Furies, and a double sun
and double Thebes appear to him; or when
Orestes, son of Agamemnon, driven   650
across the stage, flees from his mother armed
with torches and black serpents; on the threshold
the awful goddesses of vengeance squat.

Discussion Questions

1. How does Dido oppose Aeneas' decision to leave Carthage? How
    does Aeneas justify his departure?

2. What kind of an example does Aeneas set for Roman citizens by
    obeying the commands of the gods?

Sources

Virgil, *The Aeneid of Virgil*, trans. Allen Mandelbaum, Berkeley, Los
    Angeles, and London: University of California Press, 1981.

Peter Levi, *Virgil: His Life and Times*, New York: St. Marten's Press,
    1998.

Strabo, "The Roman Empire," from *The Geography of Strabo*

Strabo was born between 64 and 50 B.C. in Amasia, a city in central
Pontus not far from the southern coast of the Black Sea. Pontus had been
a satrapy of the Persian Empire before undergoing a process of
Hellenization under the kings of the Pontic dynasty. By the first century
B.C., the Romans had taken note of the growing power of the kingdom and
soon challenged its power during the Mithridatic wars. Pontus became a
Roman province around the time of Strabo's birth. The region's conquest
by the Romans directly affected Strabo's family, which had enjoyed a
prominent position in the court of the now-conquered king of Pontus. His
family appears to have cooperated with the Romans and became Roman
citizens as a result. The young man received an education befitting his
family's rank. In the Greek tradition of letters, his teachers taught him
Homeric studies, grammar, rhetoric, philosophy, and of course, geography.
That education entailed traveling to study with famous scholars and
teachers in intellectual centers in Asia Minor and even Rome. Strabo's
breadth of knowledge, demonstrated in his Geography, reflects not only
his education but also his wide-ranging curiosity on subjects as diverse as
botany, history, and philosophy.

Strabo claimed to have traveled more widely than other geographers,
a contention that served to bolster his expertise in the field. His education
had first introduced him to traveling; he continued the pursuit for the rest
of his life, sometimes for pragmatic reasons but often out of sheer
curiosity. After becoming familiar with Asia Minor, Strabo then traveled
to Europe and later Africa. He visited Greece and some of the Greek
islands on his way to the Italian peninsula, and even explored the most
famous sites in Egypt. He also commented on numerous sites that he had
not visited personally, but knew of from other travelers or accounts. The
prolific geographer straddled the line between Greek and Roman

civilizations. Although he remained very much a Greek man of letters, his ability to travel so widely owed much to the peace brought by the Romans. In his *Geography,* Strabo depicts the physical lay of the land, the people, their commerce and aptitudes, as well as the flora and fauna of the regions with which he had become familiar. In the passage below, Strabo describes the Romans and the geography of the Italian peninsula in some detail. He also observes the breadth and width of the Roman Empire and the special qualities of the Romans themselves that contributed to their successes in conquering the lands in which he had traveled.

THE GEOGRAPHY OF STRABO

The Roman Empire

CHAPTER IV.

So great indeed is Italy, and much as we have described it; we will now advert to the chief of the many things that have been described, which have conduced to raise the Romans to so great a height of prosperity. One point is its insular position, by which it is securely guarded, the seas forming a natural protection around it with the exception of a very inconsiderable frontier, which too is fortified by almost impassable mountains. A second is, that there are but few harbours, and those few capacious and admirably situated. These are of great service both for enterprises against foreign places, and also in case of invasions undertaken against the country, and the reception of abundant merchandise. And a third, that it is situated so as to possess many advantages of atmosphere and temperature of climate, in which both animals and plants, and in fact all things available for sustaining life, may be accommodated with every variety both of mild and severe temperature; its length stretches in a direction north and south. Sicily, which is extensive, may be looked upon as an addition to its length, for we cannot consider it in any other light than as a part of it. The salubrity or severity of the atmosphere of different countries, is estimated by the amount of cold or heat, or the degrees of temperature between those extremes; in this way we shall find that Italy, which is situated in the medium of both the extremes, and having so great a length, largely participates in a salubrious atmosphere, and that in many respects. This advantage is still secured to it in another way, for the chain of the Apennines extending through its whole length, and leaving on each side plains and fruitful hills, there is no district which does not participate in the advantages of the best productions both of hill and plain. We must also enumerate the magnitude and number of its rivers and lakes, and the springs of hot and cold waters supplied by nature in various localities for the restoration of health; and in addition to these, its great wealth in mines of all the metals, abundance of timber, and excellent food both for man and for beasts of all kinds.

Italy, likewise, being situated in the very midst of the greatest nations, I allude to Greece and the best provinces of Asia, is naturally in a position to gain the ascendency, since she excels the circumjacent countries both in the valour of her population and in extent of territory, and by being in proximity to them seems to have been ordained to bring them into subjection without difficulty.

If, in addition to our description of Italy, a few words should be summarily added about the Romans who have possessed themselves of it, and prepared it as a centre from whence to enforce their universal dominion, we would offer the following.—The Romans, after the foundation of their state, discreetly existed as a kingdom for many years, till Tarquin, the last [Roman king], abused his power, when they expelled him, and established a mixed form of government, being a modification both of the monarchical and aristocratical systems; they admitted both the Sabines and Latins into their alliance, but as neither they nor the other neighbouring states continued to act with good faith towards them at all times, they were under the necessity of aggrandizing themselves by the dismemberment of their neighbours. Having thus, by degrees, arrived at a state of considerable importance, it chanced that they lost their city suddenly, contrary to the expectation of all men, and again recovered the same contrary to all expectation. This took place, according to Polybius, in the nineteenth year after the naval engagement of Ægos-potami, about the time of the conclusion of the peace of Antalcidas. Having escaped these misfortunes, the Romans first reduced all the Latins to complete obedience, they then subdued the Tyrrheni, and stayed the Kelts, who border the Po, from their too frequent and licentious forays; then the Samnites, and after them they conquered the Tarentines and Pyrrhus, and presently after the remainder of what is now considered as Italy, with the exception of the districts on the Po. While these still remained a subject of dispute they passed over into Sicily, and having wrested that island from the Carthaginians they returned to complete the conquest of the people dwelling along the Po. While this war was still in hand Hannibal entered Italy, thus the second war against the Carthaginians ensued, and after a very short interval the third, in which Carthage was demolished. At the same time the Romans became masters of Africa, and of such portions of Spain as they won from the Carthaginians. Both the Greeks and the Macedonians, and the nations of Asia who dwelt on the hither side of the river Kisil-Irmak and the Taurus, took part in these struggles with the Carthaginians: over these Antiochus was king, and Philip and Perseus, these therefore the Romans found themselves obliged to subdue. The people likewise of Illyria and Thrace, who were next neighbours to the Greeks and Macedonians, at this time commenced the war with the Romans that never ceased, until the subjugation of all the people who inhabit the countries on the hither side of the Danube and the Kisil-Irmak had been effected. The Iberians, and Kelts, and all the rest who are subject to the Romans, shared a similar fate, for the Romans never rested in the subjugation of the land to their sway until they had entirely overthrown it: in the first instance they took Numantia, and subdued Viriathus, and afterwards vanquished Sertorius, and last of all the Cantabrians, who were brought to subjection by Augustus Cæsar. Likewise the whole of Gaul both within and beyond the Alps with Liguria were annexed at first by a partial occupation, but subsequently divus Cæsar and then Augustus subdued them completely in open war, so that now the Romans direct their expeditions against the Germans from these countries as the most convenient rendezvous, and have already adorned their own country with several triumphs over them. Also in Africa all that did not belong to the Carthaginians has been left to the charge of kings owning dependence on the Roman state, while such as have attempted to assert their independence have been overpowered. At the present moment both Maurusia and much of the rest of Africa have fallen to the portion of Juba on account of his good will and friendship towards the Romans. The like things have taken place in Asia. At first it was governed by kings who were dependent on the Romans, and afterwards when their several lines of succession failed, as of that of the kings Attalus, the kings of the Syrians, the Paphlagonians, Cappadocians, and Egyptians, [or] when they revolted and were subsequently deposed, as it happened in the case of Mithridates Eupator, and Cleopatra of Egypt, the whole of their territories within the Phasis and the Euphrates, with the exception of some tribes of Arabs, were brought completely under the dominion of the Romans and the dynasties set up by them. The Armenians and the people who lie beyond Colchis, both the Albani and Iberians, require nothing more than that Roman governors should be sent among them, and they would be easily ruled; their attempted insurrections are merely the consequence of the want of attention from the Romans, who are so much occupied elsewhere: the like may be asserted of those who dwell

77

beyond the Danube, and inhabit the banks of the Euxine, excepting only those who dwell on the Bosphorus and the Nomades; of these the former are in subjection to the Romans, and the latter are unprofitable for commerce on account of their wandering life, and only require to be watched. The rest of the countries [of Asia] are chiefly inhabited by Scenites and Nomades who dwell at a great distance. The Parthians indeed border on them and are very powerful, but they have yielded so far to the superiority of the Romans and our emperors, that they have not only sent back to Rome the trophies which they had at a still more distant period taken from the Romans, but Phraates has even sent his sons and his sons' sons to Augustus Cæsar, as hostages, assiduously courting his friendship: indeed the [Parthians] of the present time frequently send for a king from hence, and are almost on the point of relinquishing all power to the Romans. We now see Italy, which has frequently been torn by civil war even since it came under the dominion of the Romans, nay, even Rome herself, restrained from rushing headlong into confusion and destruction by the excellence of her form of government and the ability of her emperors. Indeed it were hard to administer the affairs of so great an empire otherwise than by committing them to one man as a father. For it would never have been in the power of the Romans and their allies to attain to a state of such perfect peace, and the enjoyment of such abundant prosperity, as Augustus Cæsar afforded them from the time that he took upon himself the absolute authority; and which his son Tiberius, who has succeeded him, still maintains, who takes his father for a pattern in his government and ordinances. And in their turn his sons, Germanicus and Drusus, who are exercising the functions of government under their father, take him for their model.

It has already been stated how this people, beginning from the single city of: Rome, obtained, possession of the whole of Italy, by warfare and prudent administration; and how afterwards, following the same wise course, they added the countries all around it to their dominion.

Of the three continents, they possess nearly the whole of Europe, with the exception only of the parts beyond the Danube, (to the north,) and the tracts on the verge of the ocean, comprehended between the Rhine and the Tanaïs (Don).

Of Africa, the whole sea-coast on the Mediterranean is in their power; the rest of that country is uninhabited, or the inhabitants only lead a miserable and nomade life.

Of Asia likewise, the whole sea-coast in our direction (on the west) is subject to them, unless indeed any account is to be taken of the Achæi, Zygi, and Heniochi, who are robbers and nomades, living in confined and wretched districts. Of the interior, and of the parts far inland, the Romans possess one portion, and the Parthians, or the barbarians beyond them, the other; on the east and north are Indians, Bactrians, and Scythians; then (on the south) Arabians and Ethiopians; but territory is continually being abstracted from these by the Romans.

Of all these countries some are governed by (native) kings, but the rest are under the immediate authority of Rome under the title of provinces, to which are sent governors and collectors of tribute; there are also some free cities, which from the first sought the friendship of Rome, or obtained their freedom, as a mark of honour. Subject to her also are some princes, chiefs of tribes, and priests, who (are permitted) to live in conformity with their national laws.

The division into provinces has varied at different periods, but at present it is that established by Augustus Cæsar; for after the sovereign power had been conferred upon him by his country for life, and he had become the arbiter of peace and war, he divided the whole empire into two parts, one of which he reserved to himself, the other he assigned to the (Roman) people. The former consisted of such parts as required military defence, and were barbarian, or bordered upon nations not as yet subdued, or were barren and uncultivated, which though ill provided with everything else, were yet well furnished with strongholds, and might thus dispose the inhabitants to throw off the yoke and rebel. All the rest, which were peaceable countries, and easily governed without the assistance of arms, were given over to the (Roman) people. Each of these parts was subdivided into several provinces, which received respectively the titles of "provinces of Cæsar" and "provinces of the People."

To the former provinces Cæsar appoints governors and administrators, and divides the (various) countries sometimes in one way, sometimes in another, directing his political conduct according to circumstances.

But the people appoint commanders and consuls to their own provinces, which are also subject to divers divisions when expediency requires it.

(Augustus Cæsar) in his first organization of (the Empire) created two consular governments, namely, (1.) the whole of Africa in possession of the Romans, excepting that part which was under the authority, first of Juba, but now of his son Ptolemy; and (2.) Asia within the Halys and Taurus, except the Galatians and the nations under Amyntas, Bithynia, and the Propontis. He appointed also ten consular governments in Europe and in the adjacent islands. Iberia Ulterior (Further Spain) about the river Bætis and Celtica Narbonesis (composed the two first). The third was Sardinia, with Corsica; the fourth Sicily; the fifth and sixth Illyria, districts near Epirus, and Macedonia; the seventh Achaia, extending to Thessaly, the Ætolians, Acarnanians, and the Epirotic nations who border upon Macedonia; the eighth Crete, with Cyrenæa; the ninth Cyprus; the tenth Bithynia, with the Propontis and some parts of Pontus.

Cæsar possesses other provinces, to the government of which he appoints men of consular rank; commanders of armies, or knights; and in his (peculiar) portion (of the empire) there are and ever have been kings, princes, and (municipal) magistrates.

Discussion Questions

1. Why, in Strabo's opinion, have the Romans sought to conquer regions outside of the Italian peninsula?

2. What kind of views does Strabo express toward the Romans as conquerors? Why might he hold those particular views?

Sources

Strabo, *The Geography of Strabo*, trans. H.C. Hamilton and W. Falconer, London: Henry G. Bohn, 1854, Vol.I 437-441 and Vol.III 295-297.

Daniela Dueck, *Strabo of Amasia: A Greek Man of Letters in Augustan Rome*, London and New York: Routledge, 2000.

CHAPTER 5

Josephus
The Antiquities of the Jews

Egeria
Diary of a Pilgramage

JOSEPHUS,
THE ANTIQUITIES
OF THE JEWS

Born not long after Caligula inherited the title of Roman emperor in
37 A.D., the Jewish historian Josephus spent his youth studying religious
and legal affairs feverishly. He claimed descent from a family of priests
that prided itself on having fought for Jewish independence for centuries.
As a teenager, he spent a few years as the disciple of an ascetic hermit
before returning to Jerusalem, where he joined the Pharisees. This Judean
faction had long resisted outside rule, and emphasized the need to keep
the Jewish religious identity pure in the face of other influences. The
Judaic kingdoms had come under Roman control after the death of Julius
Caesar in 44 B.C.

In 66 A.D., a radical faction led a revolt against Roman rule.
Josephus joined a group of priest who supported the movement for
independence. The failure of the various factions to unify in the face of
Roman dominance led to their defeat. Josephus surrendered, and as the
Romans transported their hostage toward Rome, the priest witnessed the
siege of Jerusalem and the destruction of the temple firsthand. Once in
Rome, the emperor Vespasian freed Josephus and granted him
citizenship. The emperor, who had ordered the siege on Jerusalem,
became the patron of Josephus. Titus, who had led the attack on
Jerusalem, and Domitian, both sons of Vespasian, continued to support
him during their tenures as emperor. The Jewish exile dedicated the rest
of his life to documenting the history of the Jews and their efforts to
establish independence.

The passage below, taken from *The Antiquities of the Jews,* chronicles
encounters between Roman administrators and the Jews dating from the
Caesar's rule. His commentary covers the collaboration of Herod with
Rome, among other incidents. Josephus also defines the main factions
among the Jews, the Pharisees, the Sadducees, and the Essenes, and lastly,

those led by Judas the Galilean. Finally, Josephus describes a few events during the life of Jesus and under the rule of the Roman governor, Pontius Pilate.

THE ANTIQUITIES OF THE JEWS

Josephus

CHAPTER 1.

HOW CYRENIUS WAS SENT BY CAESAR TO MAKE A TAXATION OF
SYRIA AND JUDEA; AND HOW COPONLUS WAS SENT TO BE
PROCURATOR OF JUDEA; CONCERNING JUDAS OF GALILEE AND
CONCERNING THE SECTS THAT WERE AMONG THE JEWS.

1. NOW Cyrenius, a Roman senator, and one who had gone
through other magistracies, and had passed through them till he had
been consul, and one who, on other accounts, was of great dignity,
came at this time into Syria, with a few others, being sent by Caesar to
he a judge of that nation, and to take an account of their substance.
Coponius also, a man of the equestrian order, was sent together with
him, to have the supreme power over the Jews. Moreover, Cyrenius
came himself into Judea, which was now added to the province of
Syria, to take an account of their substance, and to dispose of
Archelaus's money; but the Jews, although at the beginning they took
the report of a taxation heinously, yet did they leave off any further
opposition to it, by the persuasion of Joazar, who was the son of
Beethus, and high priest; so they, being over-pesuaded by Joazar's
words, gave an account of their estates, without any dispute about it.
Yet was there one Judas, a Gaulonite, (1) of a city whose name was
Gamala, who, taking with him Sadduc, (2) a Pharisee, became zealous
to draw them to a revolt, who both said that this taxation was no better
than an introduction to slavery, and exhorted the nation to assert their
liberty; as if they could procure them happiness and security for what
they possessed, and an assured enjoyment of a still greater good, which
was that of the honor and glory they would thereby acquire for
magnanimity. They also said that God would not otherwise be assisting
to them, than upon their joining with one another in such councils as
might be successful, and for their own advantage; and this especially, if
they would set about great exploits, and not grow weary in executing
the same; so men received what they said with pleasure, and this bold

attempt proceeded to a great height. All sorts of misfortunes also sprang from these men, and the nation was infected with this doctrine to an incredible degree; one violent war came upon us after another, and we lost our friends which used to alleviate our pains; there were also very great robberies and murder of our principal men. This was done in pretense indeed for the public welfare, but in reality for the hopes of gain to themselves; whence arose seditions, and from them murders of men, which sometimes fell on those of their own people, (by the madness of these men towards one another, while their desire was that none of the adverse party might be left,) and sometimes on their enemies; a famine also coming upon us, reduced us to the last degree of despair, as did also the taking and demolishing of cities; nay, the sedition at last increased so high, that the very temple of God was burnt down by their enemies' fire. Such were the consequences of this, that the customs of our fathers were altered, and such a change was made, as added a mighty weight toward bringing all to destruction, which these men occasioned by their thus conspiring together; for Judas and Sadduc, who excited a fourth philosophic sect among us, and had a great many followers therein, filled our civil government with tumults at present, and laid the foundations of our future miseries, by this system of philosophy, which we were before unacquainted withal, concerning which I will discourse a little, and this the rather because the infection which spread thence among the younger sort, who were zealous for
it, brought the public to destruction.

2. The Jews had for a great while had three sects of philosophy peculiar to themselves; the sect of the Essens, and the sect of the Sadducees, and the third sort of opinions was that of those called Pharisees; of which sects, although I have already spoken in the second book of the Jewish War, yet will I a little touch upon them now.

3. Now, for the Pharisees, they live meanly, and despise delicacies in diet; and they follow the conduct of reason; and what that prescribes to them as good for them they do; and they think they ought earnestly to strive to observe reason's dictates for practice. They also pay a respect to such as are in years; nor are they so bold as to contradict them in any thing which they have introduced; and when they determine that all things are done by fate, they do not take away the freedom from men of acting as they think fit; since their notion is, that

it hath pleased God to make a temperament, whereby what he wills is done, but so that the will of man can act virtuously or viciously. They also believe that souls have an immortal rigor in them, and that under the earth there will be rewards or punishments, according as they have lived virtuously or viciously in this life; and the latter are to be detained in an everlasting prison, but that the former shall have power to revive and live again; on account of which doctrines they are able greatly to persuade the body of the people; and whatsoever they do about Divine worship, prayers, and sacrifices, they perform them according to their direction; insomuch that the cities give great attestations to them on account of their entire virtuous conduct, both in the actions of their lives and their discourses also.

4. But the doctrine of the Sadducees is this: That souls die with the bodies; nor do they regard the observation of any thing besides what the law enjoins them; for they think it an instance of virtue to dispute with those teachers of philosophy whom they frequent: but this doctrine is received but by a few, yet by those still of the greatest dignity. But they are able to do almost nothing of themselves; for when they become magistrates, as they are unwillingly and by force sometimes obliged to be, they addict themselves to the notions of the Pharisees, because the multitude would not otherwise bear them.

5. The doctrine of the Essenes is this: That all things are best ascribed to God. They teach the immortality of souls, and esteem that the rewards of righteousness are to be earnestly striven for; and when they send what they have dedicated to God into the temple, they do not offer sacrifices (3) because they have more pure lustrations of their own; on which account they are excluded from the common court of the temple, but offer their sacrifices themselves; yet is their course of life better than that of other men; and they entirely addict themselves to husbandry. It also deserves our admiration, how much they exceed all other men that addict themselves to virtue, and this in righteousness; and indeed to such a degree, that as it hath never appeared among any other men, neither Greeks nor barbarians, no, not for a little time, so hath it endured a long while among them. This is demonstrated by that institution of theirs, which will not suffer any thing to hinder them from having all things in common; so that a rich man enjoys no more of his own wealth than he who hath nothing at all. There are about four thousand men that live in this way, and neither marry wives, nor are

desirous to keep servants; as thinking the latter tempts men to be unjust, and the former gives the handle to domestic quarrels; but as they live by themselves, they minister one to another. They also appoint certain stewards to receive the incomes of their revenues, and of the fruits of the ground; such as are good men and priests, are to get their corn and their food ready for them. They none of them differ from others of the Essenes their way of living, but do the most resemble those Dacae who are called *Polistae* (4) [dwellers in cities].

6. But of the fourth sect of Jewish philosophy, Judas the Galilean was the author. These men agree in all other things with the Pharisaic notions; but they have an inviolable attachment to liberty, and say that God is to be their only Ruler and Lord. They also do not value dying any kinds of death, nor indeed do they heed the deaths of their relations and friends, nor can any such fear make them call any man lord. And since this immovable resolution of theirs is well known to a great many, I shall speak no further about that matter; nor am I afraid that any thing I have said of them should be disbelieved, but rather fear, that what I have said is beneath the resolution they show when they undergo pain. And it was in Gessius Florus's time that the nation began to grow mad with this distemper, who was our procurator, and who occasioned the Jews to go wild with it by the abuse of his authority, and to make them revolt from the Romans. And these are the sects of Jewish philosophy.

CHAPTER 2.

NOW HEROD AND PHILIP BUILT SEVERAL CITIES IN HONOR OF CAESAR. CONCERNING THE SUCCESSION OF PRIESTS AND PROCURATORS; AS ALSO WHAT BEFELL PHRAATES AND THE PARTHIANS.

1. WHEN Cyrenius had now disposed of Archelaus's money, and when the taxings were come to a conclusion, which were made in the thirty-seventh year of Caesar's victory over Antony at Actium, he deprived Joazar of the high priesthood, which dignity had been conferred on him by the multitude, and he appointed Ananus, the son of Seth, to be high priest; while Herod and Philip had each of them received their own tetrarchy, and settled the affairs thereof Herod also built a wall about Sepphoris, (which is the security of all Galilee,) and

made it the metropolis of the country. He also built a wall round Betharamphtha, which was itself a city also, and called it Julias, from the name of the emperor's wife. When Philip also had built Paneas, a city at the fountains of Jordan, he named it Cesarea. He also advanced the village Bethsaids, situate at the lake of Gennesareth, unto the dignity of a city, both by the number of inhabitants it contained, and its other grandeur, and called it by the name of Julias, the same name with Caesar's daughter.

2. As Coponius, who we told you was sent along with Cyrenius, was exercising his office of procurator, and governing Judea, the following accidents happened. As the Jews were celebrating the feast of unleavened bread, which we call the Passover, it was customary for the priests to open the temple-gates just after midnight. When, therefore, those gates were first opened, some of the Samaritans came privately into Jerusalem, and threw about dead men's bodies, in the cloisters; on which account the Jews afterward excluded them out of the temple, which they had not used to do at such festivals; and on other accounts also they watched the temple more carefully than they had formerly done. A little after which accident Coponius returned to Rome, and Marcus Ambivius came to be his successor in that government; under whom Salome, the sister of king Herod, died, and left to Julia, [Caesar's wife,] Jamnia, all its toparchy, and Phasaelis in the plain, and Arehelais, where is a great plantation of palm trees, and their fruit is excellent in its kind. After him came Annius Rufus, under whom died Caesar, the second emperor of the Romans, the duration of whose reign was fifty-seven years, besides six months and two days (of which time Antonius ruled together with him fourteen years; but the duration of his life was seventy-seven years); upon whose death Tiberius Nero, his wife Julia's son, succeeded. He was now the third emperor; and he sent Valerius Gratus to be procurator of Judea, and to succeed Annius Rufus. This man deprived Ananus of the high priesthood, and appointed Ismael, the son of Phabi, to be high priest. He also deprived him in a little time, and ordained Eleazar, the son of Ananus, who had been high priest before, to be high priest; which office, when he had held for a year, Gratus deprived him of it, and gave the high priesthood to Simon, the son of Camithus; and when he had possessed that dignity no longer than a year, Joseph Caiaphas was made his successor. When Gratus had done those things, he went back to Rome, after he had

tarried in Judea eleven years, when Pontius Pilate came as his successor.

3. And now Herod the tetrarch, who was in great favor with Tiberius, built a city of the same name with him, and called it Tiberias. He built it in the best part of Galilee, at the lake of Gennesareth. There are warm baths at a little distance from it, in a village named Emmaus. Strangers came and inhabited this city; a great number of the inhabitants were Galileans also; and many were necessitated by Herod to come thither out of the country belonging to him, and were by force compelled to be its inhabitants; some of them were persons of condition. He also admitted poor people, such as those that were collected from all parts, to dwell in it. Nay, some of them were not quite free-men, and these he was benefactor to, and made them free in great numbers; but obliged them not to forsake the city, by building them very good houses at his own expenses, and by giving them land also; for he was sensible, that to make this place a habitation was to transgress the Jewish ancient laws, because many sepulchers were to be here taken away, in order to make room for the city Tiberias (5) whereas our laws pronounce that such inhabitants are unclean for seven days. (6)

4. About this time died Phraates, king of the Parthians, by the treachery of Phraataces his son, upon the occasion following: When Phraates had had legitimate sons of his own, he had also an Italian maid-servant, whose name was Thermusa, who had been formerly sent to him by Julius Caesar, among other presents. He first made her his concubine; but he being a great admirer of her beauty, in process of time having a son by her, whose name was Phraataces, he made her his legitimate wife, and had a great respect for her. Now she was able to persuade him to do any thing that she said, and was earnest in procuring the government of Parthia for her son; but still she saw that her endeavors would not succeed, unless she could contrive how to remove Phraates's legitimate sons [out of the kingdom;] so she persuaded him to send those his sons as pledges of his fidelity to Rome; and they were sent to Rome accordingly, because it was not easy for him to contradict her commands. Now while Phraataces was alone brought up in order to succeed in the government, he thought it very tedious to expect that government by his father's donation [as his successor]; he therefore formed a treacherous design against his father,

by his mother's assistance, with whom, as the report went, he had criminal conversation also. So he was hated for both these vices, while his subjects esteemed this [wicked] love of his mother to be no way inferior to his parricide; and he was by them, in a sedition, expelled out of the country before he grew too great, and died. But as the best sort of Parthians agreed together that it was impossible they should be governed without a king, while also it was their constant practice to choose one of the family of Arsaces, [nor did their law allow of any others; and they thought this kingdom had been sufficiently injured already by the marriage with an Italian concubine, and by her issue,] they sent ambassadors, and called Orodes [to take the crown]; for the multitude would not otherwise have borne them; and though he was accused of very great cruelty, and was of an untractable temper, and prone to wrath, yet still he was one of the family of Arsaces. However, they made a conspiracy against him, and slew him, and that, as some say, at a festival, and among their sacrifices; (for it is the universal custom there to carry their swords with them;) but, as the more general report is, they slew him when they had drawn him out a hunting. So they sent ambassadors to Rome, and desired they would send one of those that were there as pledges to be their king. Accordingly, Vonones was preferred before the rest, and sent to them (for he seemed capable of such great fortune, which two of the greatest kingdoms under the sun now offered him, his own and a foreign one). However, the barbarians soon changed their minds, they being naturally of a mutable disposition, upon the supposal that this man was not worthy to be their governor; for they could not think of obeying the commands of one that had been a slave, (for so they called those that had been hostages,) nor could they bear the ignominy of that name; and this was the more intolerable, because then the Parthians must have such a king set over them, not by right of war, but in time of peace. So they presently invited Artabanus, king of Media, to be their king, he being also of the race of Arsaces. Artabanus complied with the offer that was made him, and came to them with an army. So Vonones met him; and at first the multitude of the Parthians stood on this side, and he put his army in array; but Artabanus was beaten, and fled to the mountains of Media. Yet did he a little after gather a great army together, and fought with Vonones, and beat him; whereupon Vonones fled away on horseback, with a few of his attendants about him, to Seleucia [upon

Tigris]. So when Artabanus had slain a great number, and this after he had gotten the victory by reason of the very great dismay the barbarians were in, he retired to Ctesiphon with a great number of his people; and so he now reigned over the Parthians. But Vonones fled away to Armenia; and as soon as he came thither, he had an inclination to have the government of the country given him, and sent ambassadors to Rome [for that purpose]. But because Tiberius refused it to him, and because he wanted courage, and because the Parthian king threatened him, and sent ambassadors to him to denounce war against him if he proceeded, and because he had no way to take to regain any other kingdom, (for the people of authority among the Armenians about Niphates joined themselves to Artabanus,) he delivered up himself to Silanus, the president of Syria, who, out of regard to his education at Rome, kept him in Syria, while Artabanus gave Armenia to Orodes, one of his own sons.

5. At this time died Antiochus, the king of Commagene; whereupon the multitude contended with the nobility, and both sent ambassadors to [Rome]; for the men of power were desirous that their form of government might be changed into that of a [Roman] province; as were the multitude desirous to be under kings, as their fathers had been. So the senate made a decree that Germanicus should be sent to settle the affairs of the East, fortune hereby taking a proper opportunity for depriving him of his life; for when he had been in the East, and settled all affairs there, his life was taken away by the poison which Piso gave him, as hath been related elsewhere. (7)

CHAPTER 3.

SEDITION OF THE JEWS AGAINST PONTIUS PILATE. CONCERNING CHRIST, AND WHAT BEFELL PAULINA AND THE JEWS AT ROME,

1. BUT now Pilate, the procurator of Judea, removed the army from Cesarea to Jerusalem, to take their winter quarters there, in order to abolish the Jewish laws. So he introduced Caesar's effigies, which were upon the ensigns, and brought them into the city; whereas our law forbids us the very making of images; on which account the former procurators were wont to make their entry into the city with such ensigns as had not those ornaments. Pilate was the first who brought those images to Jerusalem, and set them up there; which was done

without the knowledge of the people, because it was done in the night time; but as soon as they knew it, they came in multitudes to Cesarea, and interceded with Pilate many days that he would remove the images; and when he would not grant their requests, because it would tend to the injury of Caesar, while yet they persevered in their request, on the sixth day he ordered his soldiers to have their weapons privately, while he came and sat upon his judgment-seat, which seat was so prepared in the open place of the city, that it concealed the army that lay ready to oppress them; and when the Jews petitioned him again, he gave a signal to the soldiers to encompass them routed, and threatened that their punishment should be no less than immediate death, unless they would leave off disturbing him, and go their ways home. But they threw themselves upon the ground, and laid their necks bare, and said they would take their death very willingly, rather than the wisdom of their laws should be transgressed; upon which Pilate was deeply affected with their firm resolution to keep their laws inviolable, and presently commanded the images to be carried back from Jerusalem to Cesarea.

2. But Pilate undertook to bring a current of water to Jerusalem, and did it with the sacred money, and derived the origin of the stream from the distance of two hundred furlongs. However, the Jews (8) were not pleased with what had been done about this water; and many ten thousands of the people got together, and made a clamor against him, and insisted that he should leave off that design. Some of them also used reproaches, and abused the man, as crowds of such people usually do. So he habited a great number of his soldiers in their habit, who carried daggers under their garments, and sent them to a place where they might surround them. So he bid the Jews himself go away; but they boldly casting reproaches upon him, he gave the soldiers that signal which had been beforehand agreed on; who laid upon them much greater blows than Pilate had commanded them, and equally punished those that were tumultuous, and those that were not; nor did they spare them in the least: and since the people were unarmed, and were caught by men prepared for what they were about, there were a great number of them slain by this means, and others of them ran away wounded. And thus an end was put to this sedition.

3. Now there was about this time Jesus, a wise man, if it be lawful to call him a man; for he was a doer of wonderful works, a teacher of

such men as receive the truth with pleasure. He drew over to him both many of the Jews and many of the Gentiles. He was [the] Christ. And when Pilate, at the suggestion of the principal men amongst us, had condemned him to the cross, (9) those that loved him at the first did not forsake him; for he appeared to them alive again the third day; (10) as the divine prophets had foretold these and ten thousand other wonderful things concerning him. And the tribe of Christians, so named from him, are not extinct at this day.

4. About the same time also another sad calamity put the Jews into disorder, and certain shameful practices happened about the temple of Isis that was at Rome. I will now first take notice of the wicked attempt about the temple of Isis, and will then give an account of the Jewish affairs. There was at Rome a woman whose name was Paulina; one who, on account of the dignity of her ancestors, and by the regular conduct of a virtuous life, had a great reputation: she was also very rich; and although she was of a beautiful countenance, and in that flower of her age wherein women are the most gay, yet did she lead a life of great modesty. She was married to Saturninus, one that was every way answerable to her in an excellent character. Decius Mundus fell in love with this woman, who was a man very high in the equestrian order; and as she was of too great dignity to be caught by presents, and had already rejected them, though they had been sent in great abundance, he was still more inflamed with love to her, insomuch that he promised to give her two hundred thousand Attic drachmae for one night's lodging; and when this would not prevail upon her, and he was not able to bear this misfortune in his amours, he thought it the best way to famish himself to death for want of food, on account of Paulina's sad refusal; and he determined with himself to die after such a manner, and he went on with his purpose accordingly. Now Mundus had a freed-woman, who had been made free by his father, whose name was Ide, one skillful in all sorts of mischief. This woman was very much grieved at the young man's resolution to kill himself, (for he did not conceal his intentions to destroy himself from others,) and came to him, and encouraged him by her discourse, and made him to hope, by some promises she gave him, that he might obtain a night's lodging with Paulina; and when he joyfully hearkened to her entreaty, she said she wanted no more than fifty thousand drachmae for the entrapping of the woman. So when she had encouraged the young

man, and gotten as much money as she required, she did not take the
same methods as had been taken before, because she perceived that
the woman was by no means to be tempted by money; but as she
knew that she was very much given to the worship of the goddess Isis,
she devised the following stratagem: She went to some of Isis's priests,
and upon the strongest assurances [of concealment], she persuaded
them by words, but chiefly by the offer of money, of twenty-five
thousand drachmae in hand, and as much more when the thing had
taken effect; and told them the passion of the young man, and
persuaded them to use all means possible to beguile the woman. So
they were drawn in to promise so to do, by that large sum of gold they
were to have. Accordingly, the oldest of them went immediately to
Paulina; and upon his admittance, he desired to speak with her by
herself. When that was granted him, he told her that he was sent by
the god Anubis, who was fallen in love with her, and enjoined her to
come to him. Upon this she took the message very kindly, and valued
herself greatly upon this condescension of Anubis, and told her
husband that she had a message sent her, and was to sup and lie with
Anubis; so he agreed to her acceptance of the offer, as fully satisfied
with the chastity of his wife. Accordingly, she went to the temple, and
after she had supped there, and it was the hour to go to sleep, the
priest shut the doors of the temple, when, in the holy part of it, the
lights were also put out. Then did Mundus leap out, (for he was
hidden therein,) and did not fail of enjoying her, who was at his service
all the night long, as supposing he was the god; and when he was
gone away, which was before those priests who knew nothing of this
stratagem were stirring, Paulina came early to her husband, and told
him how the god Anubis had appeared to her. Among her friends, also,
she declared how great a value she put upon this favor, who partly
disbelieved the thing, when they reflected on its nature, and partly
were amazed at it, as having no pretense for not believing it, when
they considered the modesty and the dignity of the person. But now,
on the third day after what had been done, Mundus met Paulina, and
said, "Nay, Paulina, thou hast saved me two hundred thousand
drachmae, which sum thou sightest have added to thy own family; yet
hast thou not failed to be at my service in the manner I invited thee. As
for the reproaches thou hast laid upon Mundus, I value not the
business of names; but I rejoice in the pleasure I reaped by what I did,

while I took to myself the name of Anubis." When he had said this, he went his way. But now she began to come to the sense of the grossness of what she had done, and rent her garments, and told her husband of the horrid nature of this wicked contrivance, and prayed him not to neglect to assist her in this case. So he discovered the fact to the emperor; whereupon Tiberius inquired into the matter thoroughly by examining the priests about it, and ordered them to be crucified, as well as Ide, who was the occasion of their perdition, and who had contrived the whole matter, which was so injurious to the woman. He also demolished the temple of Isis, and gave order that her statue should be thrown into the river Tiber; while he only banished Mundus, but did no more to him, because he supposed that what crime he had committed was done out of the passion of love. And these were the circumstances which concerned the temple of Isis, and the injuries occasioned by her priests. I now return to the relation of what happened about this time to the Jews at Rome, as I formerly told you I would.

5. There was a man who was a Jew, but had been driven away from his own country by an accusation laid against him for transgressing their laws, and by the fear he was under of punishment for the same; but in all respects a wicked man. He, then living at Rome, professed to instruct men in the wisdom of the laws of Moses. He procured also three other men, entirely of the same character with himself, to be his partners. These men persuaded Fulvia, a woman of great dignity, and one that had embraced the Jewish religion, to send purple and gold to the temple at Jerusalem; and when they had gotten them, they employed them for their own uses, and spent the money themselves, on which account it was that they at first required it of her. Whereupon Tiberius, who had been informed of the thing by Saturninus, the husband of Fulvia, who desired inquiry might be made about it, ordered all the Jews to be banished out of Rome; at which time the consuls listed four thousand men out of them, and sent them to the island Sardinia; but punished a greater number of them, who were unwilling to become soldiers, on account of keeping the laws of their forefathers. (11) Thus were these Jews banished out of the city by the wickedness of four men.

Discussion Questions

1. What kind of a relationship does Josephus portray between Rome and the Jews? How might his relationship to the Roman emperors who patronized his literary efforts have shaped his assessment?

2. What can we learn of the relationship between early Christianity and Judaism from Josephus' writings?

Sources

Josephus, *The Works of Josephus: Complete and Unabridged*, trans. William Whiston, Hendrickson Publishers, 1987.

Steve Mason, *Flavius Josephus: Translation and Commentary*, Vol. 9, *The Life of Josephus*, Leiden, Boston and Köln: Brill, 2001.

Egeria, *Diary of a Pilgrimage*

In the late fourth or early fifth century, a woman named Egeria undertook an extraordinary pilgrimage that led her to Syria, Palestine, and Egypt. Very little is known about her except that she probably came from northwestern Spain and may have belonged to a group of consecrated virgins. Her pilgrimage must have been lengthy, given that she spent three years in Jerusalem along the way. Egeria traveled with a retinue of attendants, was greeted with respect and enthusiasm by local clergy and monks, and was granted an armed escort in more dangerous territories, all of which indicate that she must also have been a woman of considerable resources and status to merit such treatment. Her journey suggests that a woman of her stature enjoyed considerable freedoms within this Christian world.

We know of Egeria primarily from a copy of the account of her travels that survived the centuries in an Italian monastery. Structured as a series of letters addressed to a group of sisters with whom Egeria shared some religious affinity, the diary is divided into two halves. In the first she recounts her journey from Mt. Sinai to Constantinople; in the second she details the rituals of worship she observes in Jerusalem. Egeria's letters take the form of the travelogue but in fact accomplish much more by conveying the narrative of her pilgrimage. She knew little of secular literature, but demonstrated a familiarity with biblical passages, especially the Old Testament. Egeria visited religious sites such as shrines and historical places mentioned in the bible, and provided her readers with considerable insight into the practices of Christianity and the spread of monasticism.

In the passage below, Egeria visits holy sites in Syria related to the biblical figures of Jacob, Rebecca, and Rachel. Then, en route to Constantinople, Egeria encounters a friend, called Marthana, who supervises a group of virgins near Selucium. Egeria may have belonged to a similar group of consecrated virgins in her homelands, indicating that the tradition of independent female religious figures of the early church had survived. After a few days of praying at this church and its shrine, Egerian continues her journey. The second section of the diary then begins, with a detailed description of how people in the east conduct their worship on a daily basis.

DIARY OF A PILGRIMAGE

Egeria

CHAPTER 21

After I had spent two days there, the bishop guided us to the well
where the holy man Jacob had drawn water for the flocks of the holy
woman Rebecca. This well is about six miles from Carrhae; and in
honor of this particular well, a holy church, very large and beautiful,
has been built beside it. When we had arrived at the well, the bishop
said a prayer, the proper passage from Genesis was read, and a Psalm
fitting to the place was sung. After a second prayer had been said, the
bishop blessed us. We even saw there, lying beside the well, the
extremely large stone which the holy man Jacob had moved away from
the well, for it is still shown even today. No one lives around the well
except the clergy of the church which is there and the monks who
have their cells nearby. What the holy bishop told us about their lives
was truly extraordinary. After we had prayed in the church, I went up
with the bishop to the holy monks in their cells. I gave thanks to God
as well as to those who very readily consented to receive me whenever
I came into their cells, and to speak those words which properly
should come from their mouths. They also generously bestowed gifts
on me and on all those who were with me, as it is the custom for
monks to give to those whom they very readily receive in their cells.

Since this place is in a large field, the bishop pointed out to me,
straight ahead, perhaps five hundred feet from the well, a very large
village, through which we went. This village, as the bishop said, was
formerly the property of Laban the Syrian, and the village is called
Fadana. He showed me in the village the tomb of Laban the Syrian,
Jacob's father-in-law; and I was also shown the place from which
Rachel stole the idols of her father. And so, in the name of God,
having seen everything, we said farewell to the holy bishop and the
holy monks who had graciously consented to guide us to this place,
and we returned by the route and through the resting stations we
had taken from Antioch.

CHAPTER 22

After I had returned to Antioch, I remained there for a whole week, until whatever was necessary for our journey had been prepared. I then set out from Antioch and, after journeying for several days, arrived in the province called Cilicia, the capital city of which is Tarsus, the same Tarsus in which I had already been on my trip down to Jerusalem. Since the shrine of Saint Thecla is located a three-day journey from Tarsus, in Isauria, it was a great pleasure for me to go there, particularly since it was so near at hand.

CHAPTER 23

I set out from Tarsus and I came to a certain city by the sea, still in Cilicia, called Pompeiopolis. From there I crossed over into the regions of Isauria, and I stayed at a city called Corycus. On the third day I arrived at a city called Seleucia of Isauria. On arriving there, I went to the bishop, a very holy man and a former monk. I also saw there in the same city a very beautiful church. Since it is around fifteen hundred feet from the city to the shrine of Saint Thecla, which lies beyond the city on a rather flat hill, I thought it best to go out there to make the overnight stop which I had to make.

At the holy church there is nothing but countless monastic cells for men and women. I met there a very dear friend of mine, and a person to whose way of life everyone in the East bears witness, the holy deaconess Marthana, whom I had met in Jerusalem, where she had come to pray. She governs these monastic cells of *aputactitae,* or virgins. Would I ever be able to describe how great was her joy and mine when she saw me? But to return to the subject: There are many cells all over the hill, and in the middle there is a large wall which encloses the church where the shrine is. It is a very beautiful shrine. The wall is set there to guard the church against the Isaurians, who are evil men, who frequently rob and who might try to do something against the monastery which is established there. Having arrived there in the name of God, a prayer was said at the shrine and the complete Acts of Saint Thecla was read. I then gave unceasing thanks to Christ our God, who granted to me, an unworthy woman and in no way deserving, the fulfillment of my desires in all things. And so, after spending two days there seeing the holy monks and the *aputactitae,* both men and women, who live there, and after praying and receiving Communion, I returned to Tarsus and to my journey.

I made a three-day stop before setting out on my journey from there, in the name of God. On the same day I arrived at the resting station called Mansocrenae, located at the base of Mount Tarsus, and I stopped there. The next day I climbed Mount Tarsus and travelled by a route, already known to me, through several provinces that I had already crossed on my journey down, that is, Cappadocia, Galatia, and Bithynia. Then I arrived at Chalcedon, where I stopped because of the very famous shrine of Saint Euphemia, already known to me from before. On the following day, after crossing the sea, I arrived in Constantinople, giving thanks to Christ our God who deigned to bestow such favor on me, an unworthy and undeserving person. Not only did He deign to fulfill my desire to go there, but He granted also the means of visiting what I desired to see, and of returning again to Constantinople.

After arriving there, I did not cease giving thanks to Jesus our God, who had deigned to bestow His grace upon me, in the various churches, that of the apostles and the numerous shrines that are here. As I send this letter to Your Charity and to you, reverend ladies, it is already my intention to go, in the name of Christ our God, to Asia, that is, to Ephesus, to pray at the shrine of the holy and blessed apostle John. If, after this, I am still living, I will either tell Your Charity in person—if God will deign to grant that—about whatever other places I shall have come to know, or certainly I will write you of it in letters, if there is anything else I have in mind. You, my sisters, my light, kindly remember me, whether I live or die.

CHAPTER 24

Knowing how pleased Your Charity would be to learn what is the ritual observed day by day in the holy places, I considered it my duty to make known to you the details. Each day before cockcrow, all the doors of the Anastasis are opened; and all the monks and virgins come down—the *monazontes* and the *parthene* as they are called here—and not only they, but laymen as well, men and women who wish to rise very early. From this hour until dawn, hymns are sung, and responses are made to the Psalms, and likewise to the antiphons; and after each hymn a prayer is said. Priests in groups of two or three, and a like number of deacons, take turns on successive days in coming at the same time as the monks, and after each hymn or antiphon they recite prayers. At the time when it begins to grow light, they start singing the morning hymns. Then you see the bishop come in with his clergy. He immediately goes into the grotto, and from within the railings he recites first a prayer for all the people; then he himself mentions the names of those whom he wishes to commemorate, and blesses the catechumens. Then, after he has said a prayer and blessed the faithful, the bishop comes out from the grotto sanctuary, whereupon all present come forth to kiss his hand, and he blesses each of them in turn as he goes out. And so the dismissal is given, and by now it is daylight.

Once again at the sixth hour, everyone returns a second time to the Anastasis, where Psalms and antiphons are sung while the bishop is being summoned. When he comes in, he does not sit down but, as before, goes immediately within the railings inside the Anastasis, that is to say, within the grotto where he had been in the early morning. As happened earlier, he first says a prayer and then blesses the faithful. And as he leaves the grotto sanctuary, everyone comes forth once again to kiss his hand. The same thing takes place at the ninth hour as at the sixth hour.

At the tenth hour, which is here called *licinicon,* or, as we say, vespers, a great multitude assemble at the Anastasis. All the torches and candles are lighted, and this makes a tremendous light. The light, however, is not brought in from outside, but is taken from inside the grotto, that is, from within the railings where night and day a lamp always burns. Vesper Psalms and antiphons as well are sung for some time, and then the bishop is called. When he comes in, he sits down, and the priests as well sit in their places. Hymns and antiphons are sung; and, when they have been completed according to the custom, the bishop rises and stands in front of the railings, that is, in front of the grotto, while one of the deacons makes a commemoration of each individual as is the custom. Every time the deacon mentions the name of someone, the many children standing about answer: *Kyrie eleison,* or, as we say: "Lord, have mercy," and their voices are legion. As soon as the deacon has finished what he has to say, the bishop first says a prayer, and he prays for everyone; and then everyone prays together, both the faithful and the catechumens. Next the deacon cries out that each catechumen, wherever he is standing, must bow his head, whereupon the bishop, who is standing, pronounces the blessing over the catechumens. A prayer is said and the deacon raises his voice anew to admonish each of the faithful present to bow his head; then the bishop blesses the faithful and the dimissal is given at the Anastasis; and everyone comes forth in turn to kiss the bishop's hand.

After this, singing hymns, they lead the bishop from the Anastasis to the Cross, and all the people go along also. When they have arrived there, first of all he says a prayer and blesses the catechumens; then he says a second prayer and blesses the faithful. Afterwards, both the bishop and the whole multitude go immediately behind the Cross, where everything just done before the Cross is done anew. Just as everyone at the Anastasis and before the Cross came forward to kiss the bishop's hand, so they do likewise behind the Cross. Numerous large glass lamps hang everywhere and there are many candelabra, not only in front of the Anastasis, but also before the Cross and even behind the Cross. This is the ritual that takes place daily on the six weekdays at the Anastasis and the Cross.

On the seventh day, however, that is, on Sunday, before the cockcrow, a whole multitude, whatever number can be accommodated in this place and as many as at Easter, gather outside in the forecourt adjoining the Anastasis, where for this reason there are lamps hanging. Fearing that they will not arrive in time for cockcrow, the people come beforehand and sit there, singing hymns and antiphons and reciting prayers after each hymn and antiphon. Because of the multitude which assembles, there are always priests and deacons ready to hold the vigil, for, by custom, the holy places are not opened before cockcrow.

As soon as the first cock has crowed, the bishop immediately comes down to the church and goes into the grotto at the Anastasis. All the doors are then opened, and the multitude goes into the Anastasis, where countless lights are already glowing. And as soon as the people have entered, one of the priests sings a Psalm and they all make the response; afterwards, a prayer is said. Next one of the deacons sings a Psalm, and again a prayer is said, whereupon a third Psalm is sung by one of the minor ministers, followed by a third prayer and a commemoration of all. When the three Psalms and prayers have been said, then the censers are brought into the grotto of the Anastasis, with the result that the whole basilica of the Anastasis is filled with odors of incense. Then the bishop stands within the railings, takes up the Gospel, and goes toward the door; there the bishop himself reads the Resurrection of the Lord. As soon as the reading of it has begun, so much moaning and groaning is heard, and there is so much weeping among all the people, that the hardest of men would be moved to tears because the Lord has endured so much on our behalf.

Once the Gospel has been read, the bishop goes out, and singing hymns they lead him to the Cross, and with him go the people. There another Psalm is sung and a prayer said. Then he blesses the faithful, and the dismissal is given. As the bishop leaves, all come forth to kiss his hand. The bishop then withdraws to his house, and from that time on all the monks return to the Anastasis to sing Psalms and antiphons until dawn, and to recite a prayer after each Psalm or antiphon. Each day priests and deacons take turns in holding the vigil at the Anastasis with the people. Among the laity there are men and women who wish to remain there until dawn, while others, not wishing to do so, return to their homes to sleep and to rest.

Discussion Questions

1. What motivated a woman like Egeria to undertake such a lengthy and arduous journey?

2. What kind of an impression does Egeria convey of Christianity and Christian worship in this period?

Sources

Egeria, *Diary of a Pilgrimage*, trans. George E. Gingras, New York and Paramus: Newman Press, 1970.

Patricia Wilson Kastner et al, *A Lost Tradition: Women Writers of the Early Church*, Washington D.C.: University Press of America, 1981.

CHAPTER 6

'Alī ibn Ridwān

On the Prevention of Bodily Ills in Egypt

'ALĪ IBN RIDWĀN,
ON THE PREVENTION OF BODILY ILLS IN EGYPT

As Islam swept across the Arabian peninsula and found converts in Egypt and northern Africa, Muslims established a fragile political unity that stretched from India to Spain by the tenth century. These conquerors found themselves heir to the scientific and literary achievements of classical learning, owing to the presence of many hellenized Christians, Jews, and Persians within their newly founded empire. In the field of medicine, scholars and physicians expanded upon the knowledge of the great classical authorities, Hippocrates and Galen. Muslim physicians displayed remarkably modern understandings of how diseases are transmitted, and even performed sophisticated surgeries upon their patients.

The medieval Islamic physician, 'Alī ibn Ridwān, was born in 998 to a family of poor bakers on the outskirts of Cairo. He practiced astrology to pay for his medical studies until he could earn a living as a doctor. He studied until the age of thirty-two, but never earned a medical degree, for lack of funds. As his reputation as a physician grew, local notables sought his advice. Although he never left his neighborhood in Cairo, he acquired real estate throughout the city, which allowed him a comfortable retirement in later years. He wrote prolifically, and often engaged in highly polemical correspondence with his contemporaries.

'Alī ibn Ridwān wrote the following treatise in response to a fellow physician from Tunisia who had inquired about the proper procedures for treating illnesses in Egypt. 'Alī ibn Ridwān argued that one must understand the temperament of Egyptians themselves in order to prescribe effective treatments. He also believed that natural causes take precedence over supernatural ones in causing diseases. In the sections below, 'Alī ibn Ridwān explores the causes of disease among Egyptians and then recommends a number of preventative measures to combat those diseases before they take hold.

ON THE PREVENTION OF BODILY ILLS IN EGYPT

'Alī ibn Ridwān

On the Causes of Pestilence

As for the indigenous Egyptian illnesses, we have said enough about the people and the causes of their illnesses. It is clear that most of their diseases are diseases of superfluities, and yellow and raw biles combine with the superfluities. The rest of the illnesses occur among the people quickly and in close succession, especially at the end of autumn and the beginning of winter.

As for epidemic illnesses, we have not discussed anything of this matter until now. The meaning of an epidemic illness is that it encompasses many people in one land at one time. One type is called *al-mawtān*, in which the mortality rate is high. Epidemic diseases have many causes that may be grouped into four kinds: a change in the quality of the air, a change in the quality of the water, a change in the quality of the food, and a change in the quality of psychic events.

The quality of the air is changed in two ways: first is its normal variation, and this does not produce an epidemic illness. I do not call this a sickness-inducing change. Second, when the change does not follow the normal course, it creates epidemic illness. It is the same with the other causes. If they change according to habit, they do not create illness. If the change is irregular, however, epidemic illness occurs. A deviation that changes the air from its customary nature takes place when the air becomes hotter, colder, damper, drier, or when a corruption mixes with it. The state of corruption may occur from a nearby or faraway place. Hippocrates and Galen said that it is not impossible that an epidemic disease may occur in the land of the Greeks because of a corruption that accumulated in Ethiopia, ascended to the atmosphere, then descended on the Greeks, and caused epidemic illness among them. The temperament of the air may also be changed from the normal when a large group of people arrives, whose long journey has ruined their bodies and whose humors have thus become bad. Much of their humors mixes with the air, and it is transmitted to the people, so that epidemic disease becomes evident.

The water may create epidemic illness if the water is excessive in its increase or decrease, or if a corrupt substance mixes with it. The people are forced to drink it, and the air surrounding their bodies is corrupted by the water as well. This corrupt substance may mix with the water, either in a nearby or distant place, when the water's course passes by a battlefield where many dead bodies are found. Or the river passes by polluted swamps, and it carries and mixes with this stagnant water.

Foods produce epidemic illness. If blight attacks the plants, prices rise and most people are forced to change their foods. If most of the people increase their consumption of these foods at one time, as at the festivals, dyspepsia increases and the people become ill. And if the pastureland and the water of the animals that we eat are corrupted, it will cause epidemic illness.

Psychic events create epidemic disease when a common fear of a ruler grips the people. They suffer prolonged sleeplessness and worry about deliverance or the possibility of trouble. As a result, their digestion becomes bad and their natural heat is changed. Sometimes, people are forced to violent action in such a condition. When they expect a famine in some years, they increase their hoarding. Their distress intensifies because of what they anticipate may happen.

All of these things produce epidemic illness in human bodies when many people in one country and at one time are subjected to them. It is evident that if an illness increases at one time in one city, a good deal of vapor arises from the ill bodies and changes the temperament of the air. When this vapor meets a body that is susceptible to illness, it makes that body sick, even if it were not directly subjected to what the other people had been exposed to. For example, if an epidemic illness occurs among the people because there is a rise in prices and a lack of food and there is among them someone who does not change his habit in what he eats and drinks, and if the rotten vapor of the sick reaches his body, which is susceptible to disease, he falls ill as well.

As set forth, epidemic illnesses take place in Egypt on account of a corruption that is not customary and befalls the air, regardless of whether the substance of this corruption is from the land of Egypt itself or from the lands that border it, such as the Sūdān, the Hijāz, Syria, or Barqah. Epidemics may result also from what befalls the Nile when its increase is excessive, whereupon the increase of moisture, as well as the decay, is greater than usual. When its inundation is very inadequate, the air becomes drier than usual, and the people are obliged to drink the bad water. A rottenness may also mix with the water that results from a war in Egypt, the Sūdān, or another place where many men die, and a vapor rises from their corpses into the air and putrifies it. The air's decay reaches the people of Egypt, or the water flows and carries the decay with it. In addition, epidemics may happen when prices become excessive and cause a change in diet, when blight besets the crops, injury occurs to the rams, or general fear or despair seizes the people.

Every one of these reasons produces an epidemic illness. The intensity of the illness is related to its originating cause. If more than one cause occur together, the illness is stronger, more intense, and swifter in its killing, as appeared in Egypt several years ago. Many wars took place then, killing a large number of the enemy as well as our own people. A great fear of the enemy and high prices befell the Egyptians. Furthermore, the inundation of the Nile was extraordinary in both its increase and decrease. Considerable decay from the dead mixed with the water, and the air surrounding them was contaminated by the decay of these things. Famine increased, and a high mortality occurred among the people. About a third of the people died from it.

The principle that we have related concerning the deviation of these things from their normal course each year escaped the attention of Ibn al-Jazzār, so that he mistakenly considered the things that conform with the temperament of Egypt to be the cause for the occurrence of epidemic illness.

A Summary of All That Has Been Said and an Addition to the Commentary on the Six Causes that Determine Health and Illness

The temperament of Egypt is hot and moist and includes an excessive humidity. The southern region of the country is the hottest, and less corruption exists in the southern water of the Nile than in the northern, especially north of al-Fustāt. An example is the people of al-Bushmūr; their disposition is grosser, and stupidity is dominant because they eat very coarse foods and drink bad water. As for Alexandria, Tinnis, and similar places, their closeness to the sea, their mildness of heat and cold, and the blowing of the east wind improve their natures and enhance their ambitions, freeing them from the coarseness and asininity of the people of al-Bushmūr. The fact that Tinnis is surrounded by the sea imposes a predominant humidity on the city and causes the effeminate character of its people. It is evident, therefore, that Egypt possesses many regions; each one is distinguished by special characteristics.

The reasons for pestilence in Egypt that Ibn al-Jazzār related are incorrect. The actual reason is the occurrence of a deviation from the normal, as we have stated. The bodies of the Egyptians and everything in their land are weak and quickly fall victim to illness. The end of autumn and the beginning of winter are the worst seasons of the year, when illness is most frequent. The capital is actually worse off than other cities in the rapid incidence of sicknesses. The customary illnesses are many, and most of them are illnesses of superfluity and putrefaction, accompanied by yellow bile and phlegm.

If these things are as we have described, it is desirable that we add a brief excursus on the six causes. The state of the body's temperament is good in the balanced air; the digestion improves because the light animal spirit that is in us becomes clear; and the natural heat spreads through the body in moderation. The air that deviates from the balance changes the bodies that are not accustomed to it but does not harm the bodies that are used to it, unless they are greatly susceptible to disease or are liable to deviate immoderately from their normal functioning.

Likewise, concerning the statement about what is eaten and drunk, if people become accustomed to specific foods and their bodies grow up with them, they fall ill when these foods are not available. Also, customary physical exercise may be a reason for good health because it dissolves the superfluities and smoky vapors that collect in the body. The limbs of one who has become habituated to physical exercise are firmer and stronger. Therefore, the peasants and all other workmen have greater strength and spirit than the people of leisure and luxury; the superfluities in their bodies are less. Moderate quiet makes bodies healthy and strong. Being excessively sedentary, however, does not allow the vapor to evaporate, so that congestion of the superfluities occurs, which causes harm to the body. For this reason, sedentary bodies become much more susceptible to illnesses. Consequently, quiet and leisured Egyptians more readily fall victims to illness. Excessive physical exercise also harms the bodies because it exhausts them and generates smoky superfluities in them.

If sleep and wakefulness are balanced, they produce and preserve health. When asleep, digestion improves because of the descent of heat to the interior; wakefulness dissolves the superfluities of digestion because of the ascent of heat to the exterior. Excessive sleep cools the body, and the superfluities increase in it; excessive wakefulness makes the body dry and spoils its digestion.

The teaching about retention and evacuation is similar, for if the superfluities retained in the body are excessive, they spoil digestion and decay rushes to them. If what is evacuated is more than what is retained, it is inevitable that this surplus is from the essence of the humors of the body itself, which are very vital to the body; consequently, their evacuation causes illness to occur. Therefore, what is retained should be equal to what is evacuated. Galen and other physicians said that in the winter many viscid, phlegmatic substances and filth gather in the body and stick fast in the stomach, the vessels, and the veins, as viscid and filthy substances stick fast in the watercourses of canals and drains. When spring begins, it dissolves these phlegmatic, viscid humors; then, it increases the amount of blood. The filth that accompanies the humors putrefies them; therefore, it is necessary to evacuate these before they change the blood. The vessels and veins should be cleansed of their recurring filth by purgative medicines.

Likewise, in the summer fierce humors and harmful filth collect in the body and remain in the bottom of the stomach, vessels, and veins. When autumn begins, the change of the air stirs them up and burns many of them. Because of this, it is necessary that they be evacuated before they cause harm to the body. Thus, it is desirable that every year the bodies be emptied in the spring and autumn, so that the vessels are cleansed of their filth and purged of the bad things that persist in them. There is one kind of purgative that should be used in the autumn and another kind that should be used in the spring. The desirable medication for evacuation in the spring should purge, to a great extent, much of the phlegm and viscid substances. The medication for emptying the body in the autumn should purge, to a great extent, much of the yellow bile and the fierce filth, because of what we have presented earlier. It is necessary that the medication of autumn also evacuates the moisture peculiar to Egypt, especially because the moistures produced in people's bodies at that time are great. These two evacuations—one in the spring and the other in the autumn—eliminate the filth that becomes congested in the bodies between the two seasons.

The psychic events, such as anger, sadness, and joy, do not create illness if they do not go beyond the proper bounds. It is desirable that the people of Egypt increase their gaiety and joy in order to strengthen the natural heat of their bodies, for the digestion improves, and the congestion in their bodies lessens.

It is evident from what we have said that every one of the six factors produces and sustains good health if its quantity and quality are well balanced. When they deviate from what is appropriate, they bring about illness. Therefore, the customary and epidemic illnesses of Egypt, and other illnesses as well, increase and decrease according to the degree of one's awareness of these factors and his negligence or attention to them. For example, whoever increases the consumption of food that produces black bile, his body is susceptible to melancholic illnesses. This is the case with the other causes. These six factors may change the temperament of man, his aging, his physical constitution, and his habits; they may affect the influence of the current season and the temperament of male and female. What we have said of these important things is sufficient.

Discussion Questions

1. What are the causes and cures of diseases proposed by 'Alī ibn Ridwān?
2. How effective do you think the counsel of 'Alī ibn Ridwān might have been in combating disease?

Source

'Alī ibn Ridwān, *Medieval Islamic Medicine: Ibn Ridwān's Treatise "On the Prevention of Bodily Ills in Egypt"*, trans. Michael W. Dols, Berkeley, Los Angeles and London: University of California Press, 1984.

CHAPTER 7

Einhard
The Life of Charlemagne

Dhuoda
Handbook for William

EINHARD,
THE LIFE OF
CHARLEMAGNE

Einhard, the contemporary biographer of Charlemagne, was born around 770 into a noble family residing near the Main River. His family sent him to be schooled at the monastery of Fulda, northeast of Frankfurt, where an abbot noticed his talents and recommended that he continue his studies at the Palace School of Aachen. The Carolingian kings had founded this institution to cultivate the manners of their courtiers while at the same time, educating them in the affairs of the court. Einhard soon made the acquaintance of the king and became close to Charlemagne and his family. Charlemagne appointed Einhard to carry out several important diplomatic missions, among them a journey to visit the pope. Einhard remained at the royal court after Charlemagne's death in 814, earning the favor of Louis the Pious, the successor to the throne. He married, but because the church did not yet intervene in such affairs, he was nevertheless made abbot of several monasteries. Around 830, he retired from Aachen, and died a decade later.

Einhard wrote his biography of Charlemagne sometime after leaving Aachen, probably between 929 and 836. His efforts to chronicle Charlemagne's life were motivated by his personal knowledge of Charlemagne, based upon over two decades of experience as an intimate of the emperor. Einhard also cites his gratitude to Charlemagne, who had been his patron, master, and friend. *The Life of Charlemagne* is likely one of the first and finest secular biographies of the Middle Ages. The manuscript proved popular among audiences at the time, judging from the number of copies that survived.

The document itself, modeled on the Roman biographies of Suetonius and the works of other Roman writers, presents Charlemagne as a great ruler, statesman, and warrior. Charlemagne's father Pepin was crowned King of the Franks by the pope in 754. Charlemagne inherited a vast empire spanning much of western Europe. His conquests further expanded the territories under his rule. In 800, Pope Leo III crowned the Frankish king emperor of the Christian west. In the later years of his reign, Charlemagne earned admiration for his administrative reforms and for encouraging a cultural flowering that came to be known as the Carolingian renaissance. In the following passages, Einhard conveys the greatness and vision of his patron by describing Charlemagne's visionary qualities of leadership as well as the admirable example the emperor set with his personal behavior. We learn of his conquests, his relations with foreign rulers, his efforts to improve his realm, his interest in matters of learning, and his piety and generosity.

THE LIFE OF CHARLEMAGNE

Einhard

15. CONQUESTS

These were the wars which the mighty King Charles planned so carefully and executed so brilliantly in various parts of the world during his reign of forty-seven years. As a result the kingdom of the Franks, which was already great and powerful when Charles inherited it from his father Pepin, was almost doubled in size. Formerly, the Frankish territory had encompassed only that part of Gaul lying between the Rhine and the Loire, the ocean and the Balearic Sea, as well as that part of Germania inhabited by the so-called East Franconians and bordering on Saxony and the Danube, the Rhine and the Saale-a river separating the Thuringians from the Sorbs-and, finally, the land of the Alemanni and Bavarians.

Through the wars described above Charles conquered first Aquitaine, then Gascony and the entire Pyrenees region as far south as the Ebro River. This river originates in Navarre and flows through the most fertile plains of Spain, emptying into the Balearic Sea beneath the walls of the city of Tortosa. Charles also added to his territory all of Italy from Aosta to Lower Calabria, where the border runs between the Beneventians and the Greeks-an area extending over more than a thousand miles. Furthermore, he incorporated Saxony-no small part of Germania and considered equal in length and twice the width of Franconia-and both Upper and Lower Pannonia,4 as well as Dacia on the other side of the Danube, Istria, Liburnia, and Dalmatia. Only the coastal towns of the latter countries he left to the emperor of Constantinople out of friend ship and in consideration of a treaty he had made with him. Finally, Charles subjugated and forced to pay tribute all of the barbarian and savage nations who inhabit Germania between the Rhine and the Vistula rivers, the ocean and the Danube. They speak almost the same language but have quite different customs and habits. The most important of these tribes are the Wiltzes, Sorbs, Abodrites, and Bohemians. With these he was forced to fight, but others, by far the greater number, surrendered without a struggle.

16. FOREIGN RELATIONS

Charles also increased the glory of his empire by establishing friendly relations with many kings and peoples. An example is his close friendship with King Alfons of Galicia and Asturias, who always insisted on calling himself Charles' vassal when sending him letters or ambassadors. Charles also secured the favor of the Scottish kings by his great generosity, so that they always referred to him as their master and called themselves his subjects and servants. To this day there exist letters sent by them which clearly express these feelings.

With King Harun of Persia, who ruled almost all of the Orient except India, he was on such friendly terms that Harun preferred Charles' goodwill to the friendship of all other kings and potentates on earth and considered Charles alone worthy of his respect and homage. At one time the king of the Franks sent messengers with offerings to the most Holy Sepulcher, the site of the Resurrection of our Lord and Savior. When they appeared before Harun to relay their master's wishes, the king not only permitted them to carry out their mission but also gave Charles the jurisdiction over this holy and blessed place. On their return Harun sent along his own messengers with precious gifts, garments, spices, and other riches of the Orient. A few years earlier Charles had asked him for an elephant and Harun had sent him the only one he owned.

The three emperors of Constantinople, Nicephorus, Michael, and Leo, also sought Charles' friendship and alliance and sent numerous legations to his court. Only when Charles assumed the title of emperor did they begin to distrust him out of fear that he would seize their lands. To allay these fears and make sure that there would be no occasion for further trouble, Charles at once concluded a firm treaty with them. But the Greeks and the Romans remained suspicious of Frankish power. Hence the Greek proverb: "Have a Frank as a friend, but not as a neighbor."

17. PUBLIC WORKS

No matter how much time and effort Charles spent on planning and carrying out campaigns to enlarge his realm and subjugate foreign nations, he still was able to begin work on a number of public projects designed to help and beautify his kingdom. Some of them he actually managed to complete. The Basilica of the Holy Mother of God in

Aachen, a triumph of the arts of construction, is quite rightly considered among the most remarkable of these. So, too, the bridge spanning the Rhine at Mainz, which is a full five hundred paces long, since the river is that wide at this point. The bridge was destroyed by fire and was not rebuilt because Charles died a year later. He had intended to replace the wooden structure with one of stone. He also began building two magnificent palaces, one near the city of Mainz close to his estate at Ingelheim, the other in Nymwegen on the Waal River, which flows south of the island of the Batavians. But his chief concern was for the churches. When he discovered one in any part of his kingdom that was old and ready to collapse he charged the responsible bishops and priests with restoring it. And he made sure that his instructions were carried out by having his agents check up on them.

He also set up a navy to withstand the attacks of the Norsemen and had the necessary ships built on the rivers which flow from Gaul and Germania into the North Sea. Since the Norsemen were continuously invading and devastating the Gallic and Germanic coasts, he placed guards and fortifications in all harbors and large estuaries where ships could enter. In this way he prevented the enemy from landing and looting. He did the same in the south along the shores of Narbonensis, Septimania, and Italy as far south as Rome to ward off the Moors who had just begun to take up piracy. As a consequence Italy was hardly touched during his reign except for the Etruscan town of Civita Vecchia, which was treacherously captured and plundered by the Moors. Gaul and Germania were likewise spared except for a few Frisian islands along the Germanic coast which were laid waste by the Norsemen.

21. TREATMENT OF FOREIGNERS

Charles liked foreigners and made every effort to see that they were well received. Often there were so many of them in his palace and kingdom that they were quite rightly considered a nuisance. But, magnanimous as he was, he was never bothered by such annoyances. For he felt that he would be rewarded for his troubles if they praised his generosity and gave him a good reputation.

25. STUDIES

Charles was a gifted speaker. He spoke fluently and expressed whatever he had to say with great clarity. Not only was he proficient in his mother tongue but he also took trouble to learn foreign languages. He spoke Latin as well as his own language, but Greek he understood better than he could speak it. At times he was so eloquent that he almost seemed verbose. He was zealous in his cultivation of the liberal arts, and respected and honored highly those who taught them. He learned grammar from the Deacon Peter of Pisa, who was then already an old man. Another deacon, Albinus, surnamed Alcuin, a man of Saxon origin who came from Britain and was the greatest scholar of his time, taught him the other subjects. Under his direction, the king spent a great deal of time and effort studying rhetoric, logic, and especially astronomy. He learned how to calculate and with great diligence and curiosity investigated the course of the stars. He also tried his hand at writing and to this end always kept writing tablets and notebooks under his pillow in bed in order to practice during spare moments. But since he had only started relatively late in life, he never became very accomplished in this art.

26. PIETY

The king practiced the Christian religion, in which he had been raised since childhood, with the greatest piety and devotion. That is why he built the beautiful basilica in Aachen and decorated it with gold and silver, candelabras, lattices, and portals of solid bronze. Since he was unable to get the columns and marble for the structure from anywhere else, he had them brought from Rome and Ravenna.

As long as his health permitted, the king attended church regularly in the morning and evening and took part in the late-night hours and morning mass. He was especially concerned that everything done in the church should be carried out with the greatest possible dignity. Often he admonished the sacristans to see to it that nothing unseemly or unclean was brought into the church or left there. He gave many sacred vessels of gold and silver and so many priestly vestments that when services were held not even the doorkeepers—the humblest in ecclesiastical rank—had to perform their duties in everyday clothes.

Charles also worked very hard at improving the quality of liturgical reading and chanting of the psalms. He himself was well versed in both, although he would never read in public or sing, except in a low voice and together with the congregation.

27. GENEROSITY

Charles was especially interested in helping the poor, and his generosity was of the kind for which the Greeks use the word *eleemosyna* (alms). But his charity was not limited to his own country and kingdom, for wherever he heard of Christians living in poverty, he would send them money out of compassion for their wretched lot, even overseas, to Syria and Egypt, as well as to Africa, Jerusalem, Alexandria, and Carthage. This was also the chief reason why he cultivated friendships with kings across the seas, so that the Christians living in need under their jurisdiction would receive some aid and succor.

Of all sacred and hallowed places, he loved the Cathedral of the Holy Apostle Peter in Rome most of all. He endowed its treasure room with great quantities of gold, silver, and precious stones. He sent its pontiffs many, indeed innumerable, gifts. During his entire reign nothing seemed more important to him than to exert himself to restore the city of Rome to its old splendor and to have the Cathedral of St. Peter not only secured and defended but, through his generosity, adorned and enriched beyond all other churches. Although he favored this church so much, he only visited it four times during his reign of forty-seven years, there to fulfill his vows and offer his prayers.

Discussion Questions

1. How does Einhard account for Charlemagne's greatness? Do you find his portrayal of Charlemagne as both a leader and a man convincine?

2. What policies did Charlemagne employ to maintain control over his great empire? What kind of relationships did he forge with potential competitors on the frontiers of his empire?

Sources

Einhard, *The Life of Charlemagne*, trans. Evelyn Scherabon Firchow and Edwin H. Zeydel, Coral Gables: University of Miami Press, 1972.

Lewis Thorpe, *Einhard and Notker the Stammerer: Two Lives of Charlemagne*, England: Penguin, 1969.

DHUODA,
HANDBOOK FOR WILLIAM

In the ninth century, a Carolingian noblewoman known as Dhuoda wrote a handbook to guide her eldest son in both worldly and religious affairs. She had married the godson of the Emperor Louis in 820s at the royal court. Her husband demonstrated considerable ambition in battle and at the royal court, and was rewarded with several important appointments. However, for unknown reasons, Bernard sent his wife to live a cloistered life in Uzès, in southwest France, where the emperor had granted him a large domain. There, on the borders of the empire, she occupied herself with the study of religious and classical texts and the upbringing of her first son, William.

Dhuoda's life spanned the disintegration of Charlemagne's great empire, which began under the rule of Louis the Pious and then accelerated as his sons inherited the vast territories so recently unified. Charles, Louis, and Lothar indulged in a brutal civil war with each other over the partition of the empire. Dhuoda's family found themselves the victim of these intrigues as well as the ambitions of their father. Bernard proved a corrupt and greedy vassal whose behavior at the court would hold grave consequences for his family.

Dhuoda bore her first son, William, in 826 while Bernard was away fighting in Spain. William was taken away in his teens to attend his father's new lord, Charles the Bald. William served as a hostage at the court to check the treasonous aspirations of Bernard. Her husband also took her second son, born in 841 and named after his father, to an unknown location shortly after his birth, possibly to protect this heir from royal harm. The loss of her children and her estrangement from her husband deeply saddened Dhuoda. She wrote her manual to guide her son in faith and feudal vassalage. Dhuoda's words demonstrate how deeply she herself embraced the patriarchal order of Carolingian society.

The family's demise reflects the chaos and violence of these years for the Frankish kingdom. Bernard was executed by Charles himself in 844, and William died in an attempt to avenge his father's death a few years later. The date of Dhuoda's death remains unknown, but given her references to ill health in the manual, she likely did not live to either of these events. In the passage below, she encourages her son to revere his father, his lord, and his lord's family. Ironically, if either William or his father had adhered to the principles espoused by Dhuoda, their fates might have been less tragic.

HANDBOOK FOR WILLIAM

Dhuoda

In the eleventh year of the imperial rule of our lord Louis, who then reigned by Christ's favor—on the twenty-ninth of June 824—I was given in marriage at the palace of Aachen to my lord Bernard, your father, to be his legitimate wife. It was still in that reign, in its thirteenth year on the twenty-ninth of November, that with God's help, as I believe, you were born into this world, my firstborn and much-desired son.

Afterward, as the wretchedness of this world grew and worsened, in the midst of the many struggles and disruptions in the kingdom, that emperor followed the path common to all men. For in the twenty-eighth year of his reign, he paid the debt of his earthly existence before his time. In the year after his death, your brother was born on the twenty-second of March in the city of Uzès. This child, born after you, was the second to come forth from my body by God's mercy. He was still tiny and had not yet received the grace of baptism when Bernard, my lord and the father of you both, had the baby brought to him in Aquitaine in the company of Elefantus, bishop of Uzès, and others of his retainers.

Now I have been away from you for a long time, for my lord constrains me to remain in this city. Nonetheless I applaud his success. But, moved by longing for both of you, I have undertaken to have this little book-a work on the scale of my small understanding-copied down and sent to you. Although I am besieged by many troubles, may this one thing be God's will, if it please him-that I might see you again with my own eyes. I would think it certain that I would, if God were to grant me some virtue. But since salvation is far from me, sinful woman that I am, I only wish it, and my heart grows weak in this desire.

As for you, I have heard that your father, Bernard, has given you as a hostage to the lord king Charles. I hope that you acquit yourself of this worthy duty with perfect good will. Meanwhile, as Scripture says, *Seek ye therefore the kingdom of God . . , and all these things shall be added unto you,* that is all that is necessary for the enjoyment of your soul and your body.

ON THE REVERENCE YOU SHOULD SHOW YOUR FATHER
THROUGHOUT YOUR LIFE.

Now I must do my best to guide you in how you should fear, love, and be faithful to your lord and father, Bernard, in all things, both when you are with him and when you are apart from him. In this Solomon is your teacher and your wisest authority. He chastises you, my son, and says to you in warning, *For God hath made the father* who flourishes in his children *honorable.* And likewise: *He that honoreth* his father shall have joy in his own children and shall enjoy a long life. He that obeyeth the father shall be a comfort to his mother. As one that layeth up good things, so is he who honors his father. He that feareth the Lord, honoreth his parents. So honor thy father, my son, and pray for him devotedly, that thou mayest be longlived upon the land, with a full term of earthly existence. Remember that thou hadst not been born but through him. In every matter be obedient to your father's interest and heed his judgment. If by God's help you come to this, *support the old age of thy father and grieve him not in his life. Despise him, not when thou art in thy strength.*

May you never do this last, and may the earth cover my body before such a thing might happen. But I do not believe that it will. I mention it not because I fear it but rather so that you may avoid it so completely that such a crime never comes to your mind, as I have heard that it indeed has done among many who are not like you. Do not forget the dangers that befell Elias's sons, who disobediently scorned the commands of their father and for this met with a bitter death. Nor should I fail to mention the tree of Absalom, who rebelled against his father and whom a base death brought to a sudden fall. Hung from an oak and pierced by lances, he ended his earthly life in the flower of his youth, with a groan of anguish. Lacking as he did an earthly kingdom, he never reached that highest of kingdoms promised to him.

What of the many more who behave as he did? Their path is perilous. May those who perpetrate such evil suffer accordingly. It is not I who condemn them, but Scripture that promises their condemnation, threatening them terribly and saying, *Cursed is he that honoreth not his father.* And again, *He who curseth his father, dying let him die* basely and uselessly. If such is the punishment for harsh, evil words alone, what do you think will happen to those who inflict real injury upon their parents and insult the dignity of their fathers? We hear of many in our times who, thinking their present circumstances unjust, consider such crimes without taking into account the past. On them and on those like them fall hatred, jealousy, disaster, and calamity, and *nourishment to their envy.* They lose rather than keep those goods of others that they seek, and they are scarcely able even to keep their own property. I say these things not because I have seen them happen, but because I have read about such matters in books. I have heard of them in the past, you hear about them yourself, and I am hearing them even now. Consider what will happen in the future to those who treat others in this fashion. But God has the power to bring even these people—if there are such—to lament their evil ways and, in their conversion, to do penance and be worthy of salvation. May anyone who behaves so ill stay away from you, and may God give him understanding.

Everyone, whoever he may be, should consider this, my son: if the time comes that God finds him worthy to give him children of his own, he will not wish them to be rebellious or proud or full of greed, but humble and quiet and full of obedience, so that he rejoices to see them. He who was a son before, small and obedient to his father, may then be fortunate in his own fatherhood. May he who thinks on these things in the hope that they will happen consider too what I have said above. Then "all his limbs" will work "in concert, peacefully."

Hear me as I direct you, my son William, and "listen carefully," follow the "instructions . . . of a father." Heed the words of the holy Fathers, and *bind them in thy heart* by frequent reading so that *years of life may be multiplied to thee* as you grow continually in goodness. For *they that wait upon* God, blessing him, obeying the Fathers and complying freely with their precepts—such men *shall inherit the land.* If you listen to what I say above and if you put it into worthy practice, not only will you have success here on this earth, but also you will be found worthy to possess with the saints what the Psalmist describes: *I believe to see the good things of the Lord in the land of the living.* So that this other land may be your inheritance, my son, I pray that he who lives eternally may deign to prepare you to dwell there.

DIRECTION ON YOUR COMPORTMENT TOWARD YOUR LORD.

You have Charles as your lord; you have him as lord because, as I believe, God and your father, Bernard, have chosen him for you to serve at the beginning of your career, in the flower of your youth. Remember that he comes from a great and noble lineage on both sides of his family. Serve him not only so that you please him in obvious ways, but also as one clearheaded in matters of both body and soul. Be steadfastly and completely loyal to him in all things.

Think on that excellent servant of the patriarch Abraham. He traveled a great distance to bring back a wife for his master's son. Because of the confidence of him who gave the command and the wise trustworthiness of him who followed it, the task was fulfilled. The wife found great blessing and great riches in her many descendants. What shall I say of the attitude of Joab, of Abner, and of many others toward the king David? " Facing dangers on their king's behalf in many places, they desired with all their might to please their lord more than themselves. And what of those many others in holy Scripture who faithfully obeyed their lords' commands? Because of their watchful strength they were found worthy to flourish in this world. For we know that, as Scripture tells, all honor and authority are given by God. Therefore we should serve our lords faithfully, without ill will, without reluctance, and without sluggishness. As we read, *there is no power but from God: and he . . . that resisteth the power, resisteth the ordinance of God.*

That is why, my son, I urge you to keep this loyalty as long as you live, in your body and in your mind. For the advancement that it brings you will be of great value both to you and to those who in turn serve you. May the madness of treachery never, not once, make you offer an angry insult. May it never give rise in your heart to the idea of being disloyal to your lord. There is harsh and shameful talk about men who act in this fashion. I do not think that such will befall you or those who fight alongside you because such an attitude has never shown itself among your ancestors. It has not been seen among them, it is not seen now, and it will not be seen in the future.

Be truthful to your lord, my son William, child of their lineage. Be vigilant, energetic, and offer him ready assistance as I have said here. In every matter of importance to royal power take care to show yourself a man of good judgment—in your own thoughts and in public—to the extent that God gives you strength. Read the sayings and the lives of the holy Fathers who have gone before us. You will there discover how you may serve your lord and be faithful to him in all things. When you understand this, devote yourself to the faithful execution of your lord's commands. Look around as well and observe those who fight for him loyally and constantly. Learn from them how you may serve him. Then, informed by their example, with the help and support of God, you will easily reach the celestial goal I have mentioned above. And may your heavenly Lord God be generous and benevolent toward you. May he keep you safe, be your kind leader and your protector. May he deign to assist you in all your actions and be your constant defender. *As it shall be the will of God in heaven so be it done.* Amen.

ON TAKING COUNSEL.

If God should someday bring you to such a point that you are found worthy to be called to the council, of the magnates, consider carefully on what; when, to whom, and how you should offer worthy and appropriate comment. Act with the advice of those who encourage you to behave loyally in body and in soul. It is written: *do everything with counsel, and thou shalt not repent when thou hast done.* Here "everything" refers not to evil deeds offensive to good judgment, but to lofty and generous actions such as enhance the health of soul and body and are beyond reproach; such deeds are useful and steady, of long-enduring effect. As someone said, *what I have said is determined.*

Those who do metalwork, when they begin to pound out gold to make it into leaf, wait for the best and most suitable day, weather, and temperature. Then the gold that they work for decoration, brilliant and sparkling even among the finest metals, may shine still more brightly. In the same way, the thought of those in council should in all matters follow the well-reasoned pattern known to the wise. For the speech of one who has good understanding is whiter than snow, sweeter than honey, purer than gold or silver. Why? Because, as Scripture says, from the mouth of a wise man comes honey. The eloquence of a great man is therefore a favor greater than silver and gold because his lips draw from the honeycomb and his words *are pure words . . . tried by the fire, purged.*

There are no riches where stupidity reigns, and nothing is wanting, nothing an obstacle, in matters where gentle speech prevails. Whoever tries to be numbered among the wise can be welcome to both God and man and pleasing in every way to his earthly lord. For he will be known as true as gold, seen as whiter than snow. Many things are clear in this secular world. For Scripture says, *and because iniquity hath abounded, the charity of many shall grow cold.* As things are now, one does not know whom to choose as a counselor or whom one ought first to believe, and for many the hope of finding help from anyone remains uncertain. Read the *Synonyms.*

But you must not despair in this, my son. There are many descended from these ancients who still, with God's help, are willing and able to give counsel that is good, welcome, and appropriate in respect to both themselves and their lords. And all these things happen through him who is called the Most High. For Scripture says, *Is there no physician in Egypt or balm in Galaad,* clear water in Canaan or counselor in Israel? There is indeed, and clear understanding reveals itself in many men. God, who gives light to the world and is the angel of good counsel, knows his own. He shows them the words that bring the soul's salvation. May he who was then among the ancients and is now among the living, who is in you, goes out from you, and returns to you, who directs you to fight alongside a worthy, high king to carry out that earthly lord's command—may that God cause you to arrive at that high, right counsel. Amen.

SPECIAL DIRECTION ON THE SAME TOPIC.

For you to be such a man depends entirely on the judgment and the power of omnipotent God. If, with the aid of the highest creator, you come to the time that I have mentioned above, fear immoral men and seek out worthy ones. Flee evil men and find good ones. Do not take counsel with a man of ill will or a weak-spirited man or a wrathful man. For he will corrupt you like tin, and under his command you will never rest secure. For the wrath and the envy that come easily to him draw him at once, headlong, to the depths.

Let not your fate be like Achitofel's or like Aman's, bad and arrogant men whose counsels were worthless and who, when they gave bad advice to their lord, fell headlong in both spirit and body to their deaths. For I wish, my son, that you take pleasure in fighting on your lord's behalf, as did such men as Doeg the Edomite and the humble Mardochai. Achitofel offered Absalom the bad counsel that he should rebel against his father, David-and Achitophel did so in order to win the son's favor. But by the will of God, Achitophel's evil counsels were brought to nothing? But Chusai and Doeg, a strong man who firmly held his ground against another determined man, remained unshakable in their counsel. On the other hand Aman, on account of the pride in his envious spirit, gave evil counsel to Assuerus so that sons of Israel were killed. But Mardochai, praying for God's help to liberate himself and his people, gave the same king good counsel, the evidence of loyalty, in order to free and to vindicate himself. Mardochai began, "Consider, O king."

By God's providence, one man merits salvation with his people. Another, a proud man, goes away empty along with all his house. He is hung on the gallows that in his envy he has prepared for the humble man, so that this evil is turned upon its designer. All by himself he has brought his life, even his body, to a worse end. There is fulfilled in him and in those like him what is said: *He hath conceived sorrow, and brought forth iniquity. He hath opened a pit . . . and fallen into it.* For he who had prepared evil for his innocent brother has now rushed headlong and straightaway into death. God, who is good and who in his goodness spares the wicked, rightly desires to bring all men to himself through penance. For *he knoweth both the deceiver, and him that is deceived* by the deceiver.

Therefore, my son William, fear immoral men and seek out worthy ones. Flee evil men like those mentioned here, but attach yourself to good men seeking after worthy goals. They offer counsel in the most useful of ways, in their true subjection to the wishes of their lords, and they are found worthy to receive fitting reward both from God and in the secular world. I pray that such counsel as has been in those great men may grow in you now, every day, always, my best of sons.

REGARDING YOUR LORD'S FAMILY.

As for the great and famous relations and associates of your royal lord—those who are descended from his illustrious father's side as well as those related to him by marriage—fear, love, honor, and cherish them if you and those who fight alongside you are found worthy to serve them in the royal arid imperial court or anywhere else you may act on their behalf. In all undertakings in their interest maintain a pure, fitting, and steadfast obedience to them, as well as good faith in the execution of your duties.

Remember how David comported himself toward Jonathan, the son of the king Saul. In every way, throughout his life, he was a pure, faithful, and true supporter of both the father and the son, and also their children, not only during their lives but also after their deaths. Even after their destruction the sweetness of his great love caused him to mourn them with sorrowful tears, greatly lamenting and saying, *How are the valiant fallen in battle and the weapons of war perished?* And also, *I grieve for thee, my brother Jonathan: exceedingly beautiful, and amiable to me above the love of women, swifter than eagles, stronger than lions.* And again, my best of children, *the arrow of Jonathan never turned back.* In these and other instances David was filled with grief for the king's son, and with his retainers he mourned deeply over Jonathan's ruin. May you and those who fight alongside you avoid such a fate.

I am having this copied out as an example for you. For when David recovered, as if consoled by the great loyalty of his love for them, he praised his dead friends in another voice, with sighing, *Saul and Jonathan, lovely, and comely in their life, even in death they were not divided.* Many who faithfully obeyed the commandments of their lords and their lords' relations are abundantly and honorably praised in sacred Scriptures. Read the book of Kings and the books of the other Fathers, and you will find many.

So, my son William, bear patiently the yoke that governs a servant and be faithful to your lord Charles—whatever sort of lord he may be—and to his worthy relations of both sexes and to all those of royal origins. It is fitting for you and for all those who fight under their royal power to do so, and I wish that you serve them to good ends, faithfully, with all your might. For as we believe, God chose them and established them in royal power, granting them glory almost as great in its likeness to the ancients' as that promised to Abraham, Isaac, and Jacob, and to their worthy children and descendants.

May the omnipotent Father—our strong King, the glorious Highest—make them peaceful and harmonious, seeking concord after the manner of their fathers in this earthly realm. Then they may shine in prosperity and rule, protect, and govern the world and its people with strength in the service of God and his saints. And they may hold and defend our people from the blows of enemies pressing all around, uniting the holy church of God the more firmly in Christ and his true religion. May they see the children of their sons pleasing God in worthy fashion, growing and flourishing, and aiming for heaven through many cycles of the years, persevering in this course until they come happily to the end of their lives. As for you, after you have reached the end of this present life, may he who gives all recompense and all bounty bring you to rest in the kingdom of heaven with those Fathers whom I have mentioned. May he bring you to his kingdom and his glory—you who struggle here to render faithful service both to your several earthly lords and to that singular Lord who gives fitting reward for your merits from his own riches. And may he unite you happily to Christ.

Discussion Questions

1. What is the relationship between faith and feudal loyalty, according to Dhouda?
2. Why did loyalty constitute such an important aspect of Carolingian society?

Sources

Dhuoda, *Handbook for William: A Carolingian Woman's Counsel for Her Son*, Lincoln and London: University of Nebraska Press, 1991.

Eleanor Duckett, *Medieval Portraits from East and West*, Ann Arbor: University of Michigan Press, 1972.

CHAPTER 8

Ramón Lull
Felix

RAMÓN LULL,
FELIX

In the decade before Ramón Lull's birth, the Spanish Christian kingdoms had accelerated their efforts to reconquer the Iberian peninsula. By the time he had become a teenager, the Muslim hold on the region had been reduced to the kingdom of Granada in the south. Born in 1232 on the island of Majorca, Lull spent the first half of his life in Palma, the capital of this Catalonian possession, where he was exposed to the cosmopolitanism of the eastern Mediterranean. Christians, Muslims, and Jews coexisted on the island, and communities of Genoese and Pisan merchants lived among the native Catalan speakers. Lull spent his youth idly, by his own estimation. He attended the courts of James I and later James II, writing poetry and love songs. He married and fathered two sons.

A conversion experience at the age of thirty changed the course of Lull's life. His visions of Jesus prompted Lull to devote himself to converting Muslims to Christianity. He learned Arabic from a slave that he had purchased, then traveled to Paris to study theology. After founding a school in Majorca, Lull journeyed to North Africa to fulfill his religious calling. In Tunis, Lull exhausted the patience of his Muslim hosts and was imprisoned for a time. He survived a shipwreck before returned to Tunis in his last years, where he preached in the streets. The local authorities executed him in 1316.

Lull wrote prolifically on a wide range of subjects. After his youthful forays in chivalric poetry, Lull turned to more serious topics. Most of his works address theological themes, the process of conversion, and debates with Muslim scholars. He strove to prove to his would-be converts that the truth of Christianity could be proved. He wrote a lengthy autobiography, and attempted two works of fiction. Lull's novels *Felix and Blaquerna* mark the birth of Catalan literature. Both are morality tales, directed at a

Christian audience rather than an Muslim one. *Felix,* written about 1288, takes as its theme the relationship between God and humanity. The main character wanders about the world seeking advice and instruction on a number of subjects ranging from heavenly beings to plants and minerals. In the passage below, Felix asks a hermit to define God for him. The hermit responds by way of an anecdote that illustrates Lull's beliefs in the power of love in the relationship between the human and the divine.

FELIX

Ramón Lull

WHAT IS GOD?

"SIR HERMIT said Felix, could you tell me what God is? For I want very much to know, since with this knowledge of what God is, my will would be uplifted to love God more than I now do, because it is only natural that through enlightened understanding the will is heightened in loving something about which the understanding has knowledge."

For a long time the hermit thought over the question Felix had asked him. While the hermit was thinking how he could make Felix understand what God was, Felix wondered why the hermit was taking so long to answer the question he had asked, and he said: "Sir, a man found a precious stone which was worth a thousand sous and which he sold for one denier to a man who knew what kind of a stone it was and was able to get a thousand sous for it. Therefore, sir, if you know what God is, I beg you to tell me so that I can love and know Him according to His true value. And if you do not know what God is, I am in great wonder at how you can love Him so much without knowledge, nor how for His sake you can undergo such a harsh life in this hermitage. And it seems to me that if you do not know what God is, then at the slightest opportunity you would disdain Him, as the man disdained the precious stone, about which he knew nothing, selling it for one denier, which denier he knew about, and because of His knowledge of the denier and ignorance of the value of the stone, he preferred having the denier to the stone."

"Dear son," said the hermit, "in a certain land there was once a woman who heard a king praised for his wisdom, power, and good customs; and because of all the good things she had heard about the king, she decided to go to that land where the king ruled. When she came before the king and saw how well-ordered was his court, and saw his great power and his good administration, and when, in addition, she saw that the king was very handsome as a person, well-mannered and full of virtues, then she felt a much greater love for the king than before, when she had not yet seen the king. And you, my fair son, have already remarked how the will loves more that which is known than that which is unknown; as for me, you should realize that I came to this hermitage in order to gain knowledge of what God is, since it is something I have long wanted to know. And in order to acquire this knowledge I have studied theology and philosophy for a long time, and in this hermitage—I am doing everything I can to understand and comprehend the essence of our Lord God."

The hermit said to Felix, "A king once had a wife who was very beautiful and good, and whom the king loved very much. That queen loved the king very much, and on account of this great love she was jealous of the king and of a certain damsel of his, with whom he enjoyed conversing because of her pleasant manner of speaking. Every day this queen was in great sorrow, and no matter what the king did or said, he could not cheer her up, a fact which caused him great wonder. The king tried as hard as he could to make her content, and finally when he saw that he could not make her happy, he began to suspect the queen and to think she was perhaps doing something to dishonor him."

"Dear son," said the hermit, "when the king became jealous and suspicious of his wife, then he began to love the queen less, and because of the queen, to love the damsel less. The king went for a long time without speaking to the damsel, and the queen began to cheer up, which cheer caused the king great wonder; for when he had formerly done everything he could to please her, he could not cheer her up, and now when he had stopped trying to please her, the queen loved him more than before. The king was in great wonder at the queen's odd ways, but he fell in with them and let himself be loved by the queen, so that she would be happy and content in her love."

"When men of this world take pleasure in temporal delights, and do not love them for the sake of the Creator who created them, so that with them and in them one learns to know and love Him, then God becomes estranged from such people, and because of this estrangement they can no longer have knowledge of Him, nor of the pleasure derived from this knowledge. But when a person ceases loving the delights of this world, through which delights and world a person can love God, then these delights and the world seek out that man, and give him a way in which he can love God and have knowledge of Him. And in this, fair son," said the hermit, "you can, in this world, have knowledge of what God is: namely, that God is that on account of which the world will take you further from loving God if you love the world for itself; and God is that on account of which the world exemplifies God if you love the world for the sake of knowing and loving God."

"Dear son," said the hermit, "a person has knowledge of God by saying that in Him there is nothing which lacks nobility, nor perfection of goodness, greatness, eternity, power, wisdom, will, virtue, and the other perfections existing in God; thus, when a person has acquired the knowledge that God is not something in which there is any defect, that person can have knowledge of God, who is the fulfillment of all goodness, of all greatness, all eternity, and similarly with power, wisdom, virtue, will, and the other dignities."

"Fair son," said the hermit, "a merchant had a thousand bezants, and he wanted to have another thousand; and when he had two thousand, he immediately wanted more, and this way he amassed a hundred thousand bezants without feeling any satisfaction in his soul. The merchant wondered greatly at this fact, and he thought that perhaps the fulfillment of his desires lay not in money but rather in the owning of castles and estates and property, which he was determined to have and which he obtained, and yet he still felt no sense of fulfillment, for the more he bought and possessed, the more his desire to own estates and castles increased. When the merchant tnultiplied his wealth and saw that it still gave him no satisfaction, he thought that he would satisfy his soul by having a wife and children. He got himself wife and children and still he was not satisfied, and he wanted honors and many other things; and the more things he had, the more his soul wanted to have. The merchant was in great wonder as to how he could satisfy his soul with anything in this world, and he finally thought of having God in his soul. He then loved and served God with what He had given him, and he felt satisfied and fulfilled, and he desired nothing more. So you should know, fair son, that God is that which, in this world, gives satisfaction to the soul of the person who loves and serves Him with all his power."

"Through a forest where a hermit lived, a fully armed knight rode past on his horse, and he came upon the hermit picking the plants on which he subsisted in that hermitage. The knight asked the hermit what God was; and the hermit replied that God is that for which all existing things were created and ordered; and God is that which will cause the good and the wicked to rise from the dead, and will give everlasting glory to the good and punishment to the wicked; and God is that which causes it to rain, which makes plants flower and bear seed, and which gives life and sustenance to everything there is. When the hermit had satisfied the knight with regard to the question he had posed, the hermit asked the knight what a knight was. And the knight replied that a knight was a man chosen to ride on horseback to carry out justice and to protect and safeguard the king and his people so that the king could reign in such a manner that his subjects could love and know God."

"Sir," said Felix, "a knight asked a good woman, daughter of chastity, to make physical love with him, and the woman asked him what love was. The knight replied that love was that which made separate wills unite toward a common end. The woman asked the knight if this love he asked of her would unite her with God in glory when she left the life of this world. The knight felt ashamed of what he had asked the woman, and he said the following: 'For a long time I have been subject to false love and in ignorance of true love.' And he said to the woman that he realized that true love united a person with God, and separated him from treachery, lust, cowardice, and all deceit and defect. Nevertheless, he still wanted to know what love was in itself, for one thing is what love does, and another is what love is; and he therefore asked the woman to give him knowledge of what love is, since she had already given him knowledge of foolish love, which he had loved without realizing what it was. The woman was very pleased by the knight's devoutness, and she praised God for having warmed him with the fire of true love, and to God she addressed the following words: 'O Lord, true and glorious God, since, through love, You have enamored this knight, I beg of You to give him knowledge of what love is, for by Your grace and virtue I have given him knowledge of what love does, but he wishes to rise higher in his understanding of love, so that he can love all the better, and he wishes to know what love is in itself.'"

After Felix had told the hermit about the words of love between the woman and the knight, he realized that Felix was not satisfied with the knowledge he had given him of God, whose being he had expressed through God's effect on His creatures, and that Felix wanted to know what God's being was in itself and in its actions. The hermit therefore said the following words to Felix:

"There was once a philosopher who had a son he loved very much and to whom he taught philosophy for many years. When his son was very knowledgeable in the science of philosophy, his father showed him a book he had written, and he asked whether his son knew that he was a man because of the fact that he had written the book or because of the fact that he was his father. The son replied that by the book he knew that he was a man, because to man belonged the ability to write; but even more he knew his father to be a man because he had engendered a man."

After this example, the hermit, told Felix that God is that to which belong actions which no one else can perform, save God alone, which actions God performs in creatures. But the way one can best know what God is in Himself, is in how God in Himself and from Himself engenders God, that is to say that God the Father engenders God who is the Son, and from the Father and the Son there issues God who is the Holy Ghost, and all three are in a single God; which God is that which is God the Father, God the Son, and God the Holy Ghost, and which is one God and not three gods. And God is that thing which is infinite, eternal, wise, volitional, virtuous, and who in Himself is the fulfillment of all goodness, all infinity, and of everything He is in Himself.

Felix was very pleased with the knowledge of God the hermit had given him, and he praised and blessed God, who had made Himself known to him; and in his soul he felt his love in loving God increase because he now understood Him better than before.

Discussion Questions

1. What is the meaning of the anecdotes related by the hermit in response to Felix's questions?
2. What kinds of messages for Christians do you discern in Lull's work?

Sources

Ramón Lull, *Selected Works of Ramón Lull (1232-1316)*, Vol II, trans. Anthony Bonner, Princeton: Princeton University Press, 1985.

J.N. Hillgarth, *Ramón Lull and Lullism in Fourteenth-Century France*, Oxford: Clarendon Press, 1971.

CHAPTER 9

Marco Polo

The Travels of Marco Polo

Boccaccio

The Decameron

MARCO POLO, "OF THE ADMIRABLE DEEDS OF KUBLAI KHAN—THE EMPEROR NOW REIGNING—AND HIS GREAT POWER," FROM *THE TRAVELS OF MARCO POLO*

In 1271, at the age of seventeen, Marco Polo set out in the company of his father and uncle, both Venetian merchants by trade, for the empire of the Great Khan, in what is today modern China. Venetian traders were unequaled in the late thirteenth century, dominating Mediterranean trading with the east for precious goods like spices, silks, feathers, dyes and slaves. Missionaries and merchants from Europe had arrived in western Asia as early as 1260, but the Polos were the first to venture further east. From one of their emporiums on the Black Sea, the elder Polos proved themselves even more enterprising and adventurous than their fellow Venetians. They had made the acquaintance of the Khan on an earlier journey for the purpose of trading jewels with the Mongols, whose reign stretched across the continent central Asia. The brothers had received an invitation from the Khan himself on that earlier visit to return to his empire.

This journey, according to Marco Polo's relation of it, took three and a half years. Twenty-four years would pass before the younger Polo returned to his homeland. Polo claimed that he quickly made himself indispensable to the Khan, earning himself a position of some favor at the royal court. The Khan, Lord of the Tartars, ruled over a huge area; he had in fact succeeded in unifying China shortly before the Polos reached his court. The Polos requested permission to return home repeatedly, but these requests were refused by the Khan for many years. The Polos finally returned home in 1295 after traveling as part of a Mongol bridal party traveling to Persia. Marco Polo published his account of the journey a few years after his return to Venice. Over the course of the next twenty-five years, the book enjoyed unparalleled popularity, and was translated into at least five languages. Polo continued to pursue family business interests, and died in 1324. On his deathbed, he confirmed that every strange and wonderful occurrence in his book was true.

In the passage below, Marco Polo describes the wonders of Kublai Khan's rule. After triumphing over a rebellious competitor, the Khan returns to the capital, where Polo observes the great ruler's policies of religious tolerance and charity. Finally, Polo tells of the religious practices and social customs of the Mongols.

THE TRAVELS OF MARCO POLO

Marco Polo

Of the Admirable Deeds of Kublai Khan—the Emperor Now Reigning—and His Great Power

CHAPTER 1

OF THE ADMIRABLE DEEDS OF KUBLAI KHAN—THE EMPEROR
NOW REIGNING—AND HIS GREAT POWER

In this book it is our design to treat all of the great and admirable achievements of the Great Khan now reigning, who is styled Kublai Khan; the latter word implying in our language Lord of Lords, and of a surety he hath good right to such a title, for in respect to number of subjects, extent of territory, and amount of revenue, he surpasses every sovereign that has heretofore been or that now is in the world; nor has any other been served with such implicit obedience by those whom he governs. This will so evidently appear in the course of our work, as to satisfy every one of the truth of our assertion.

CHAPTER 6

OF THE RETURN OF THE GREAT KHAN TO THE CITY OF
KANBALU AFTER HIS VICTORY, AND OF THE HONOUR HE CONFERS
ON THE CHRISTIANS AND THE JEWS, AND OTHER SUBJECTS

The Great Khan, having obtained this signal victory, returned with great pomp and triumph to the capital city of Kanbalu [Peking]. This took place in the month of November, and he continued to reside there during the months of February and March, in which latter was our festival of Easter. Being aware that this was one of our principal solemnities, he commanded all the Christians to attend him, and to bring with them their Book, which contains the four Gospels of the Evangelists.

After causing it to be repeatedly perfumed with incense, in a ceremonious manner, he devoutly kissed it, and directed that the same should be done by all his nobles who were present. This was his usual practice upon each of the principal Christian festivals, such as Easter and Christmas; and he observed the same at the festivals of the Saracens, Jews, and idolaters.

Upon being asked his motive for this conduct, he said: "There are four great Prophets who are reverenced and worshipped by the different classes of mankind. The Christians regard Jesus Christ as their divinity; the Saracens, Mahomet; the Jews, Moses; and the idolaters, Sogomom-bar-kan, the most eminent amongst their idols. I do honour and show respect to all the four, and invoke to my aid whichever amongst them is in truth Supreme in Heaven." But from the manner in which his majesty acted towards them, it is evident that he regarded the faith of the Christians as the truest and the best; nothing, as he observed, being enjoined to its professors that was not filled with virtue and holiness.

By no means, however, would he permit them to bear the cross before them in their processions, because upon it so exalted a personage as Christ had been scourged and put to death. It may perhaps be asked by some, why, if he showed such a preference to the faith of Christ, he did not conform to it, and become a Christian?

His reason for not so doing, he assigned to Nicolo and Mafeo Polo, when, upon the occasion of his sending them as his ambassadors to the Pope, they ventured to address a few words to him on the subject of Christianity. "Wherefore," he said, "should I become a Christian? You yourselves must perceive that the Christians of these countries are ignorant, inefficient persons, who do not possess the faculty of performing anything miraculous; whereas you see that the idolaters can do whatever they will. When I sit at table the cups that were in the middle of the hall come to me filled with wine and other beverage, spontaneously and without being touched by human hand, and I drink from them. They have the power of controlling bad weather and obliging it to retire to any quarter of the heavens, with many other wonderful gifts of that nature. You are witnesses that their idols have the faculty of speech, and predict whatever is required.

"Should I become a convert to the faith of Christ, and profess myself a Christian, the nobles of my court and other persons who do not incline to that religion will ask me what sufficient motives have caused me to receive baptism, and to embrace Christianity. 'What extraordinary powers,' they will say, 'what miracles have been displayed by its ministers? Whereas the idolaters declare that what they exhibit is performed through their own sanctity, and the influence of their idols?'

"To this I shall not know what answer to make, and I shall be considered by them as labouring under a grievous error, whilst the idolaters, who by means of their profound art can effect such wonders, may without difficulty compass my death. But return you to your pontiff, and request of him, in my name, to send hither a hundred persons well skilled in your law, who being confronted with the idolaters shall have power to restrain them, and showing that they themselves are endowed with similar art, but which they refrain from exercising, because it is derived from the agency of evil spirits, shall compel them to desist from practices of such a nature in their presence. When I am witness of this, I shall place them and their religion under a ban, and shall allow myself to be baptized. Following my example, all my nobility will then in like manner receive baptism, and this will be imitated by my subjects in general. In the end the Christians of these parts will exceed in number those who inhabit your own country."

From this discourse it must be evident that if the Pope had sent out persons duly qualified to preach the gospel, the Great Khan would have embraced Christianity, for which, it is certainly known, he had a strong predilection.

CHAPTER 27

OF THE RELIEF AFFORDED BY THE EMPEROR TO ALL THE PROVINCES OF HIS EMPIRE IN TIMES OF DEARTH OR MORTALITY OF CATTLE

The Great Khan sends every year his commissioners to ascertain whether any of his subjects have suffered in their crops from unfavourable weather, from storms of wind or violent rains, or by locusts, worms, or any other plague; and in such cases he not only refrains from exacting the usual tribute of that year, but furnishes them from his granaries with so much corn as is necessary for their subsistence, as well as for sowing their land.

With this view, in times of great plenty, lie causes large purchases to be made of such kinds of grain as are most serviceable to them, which is stored in granaries provided for the purpose in the several provinces, and managed with such care as to ensure its keeping for three or four years without damage. It is his command, that these granaries be always kept full, in order to provide against times of scarcity; and when, in such seasons, he disposes of the grain for money, he requires for four measures no more than the purchaser would pay for one measure in the market. In like manner where there has been a mortality of cattle in any district, he makes good the loss to the sufferers from those belonging to himself, which he has received as his tenth of produce in other provinces. All his thoughts, indeed, are directed to the important object of assisting the people whom he governs, that they may be enabled to live by their labour and improve their substance. We must not omit to notice a peculiarity of the Great Khan, that where an accident has happened by lightning to any herd of cattle, flock of sheep, or other domestic animals, whether the property of one or more persons, and however large the herd may be, he does not demand the tenth of the increase of such cattle during three years; and so also if a ship laden with merchandise has been struck by lightning, he does not collect from her any custom or share of her cargo, considering the accident as an ill omen. God, he says, has shown himself to be displeased with the owner of the goods, and he is unwilling that property bearing the mark of divine wrath should enter his treasury.

CHAPTER 31

OF THE GREAT AND ADMIRABLE LIBERALITY EXERCISED BY THE GREAT KHAN TOWARDS THE POOR

It has been already stated that the Emperor distributes large quantities of grain to his subjects. We shall now speak of his great charity to and provident care of the poor in the city of Kanbalu. Upon his being informed of any respectable family, that had once lived in easy circumstances and by misfortunes reduced to poverty, or who, in consequence of infirmities, are unable to work for their living or to raise a supply of any kind of grain: to a family in that situation he gives what is necessary for their year's consumption. At the customary period they present themselves before the officers who manage this department of his Majesty's expenses and who reside in a palace where that business is transacted. Here they deliver a statement in writing of the quantity furnished to them in the preceding year, according to which they receive also for the present.

In a similar way the Emperor provides clothing for his poor, which he has the means of doing from his tenths of wool, silk, and hemp. These materials he has woven into the different sorts of cloth, in a house erected for that purpose, where every artisan is obliged to work one day in the week for his Majesty's service. Garments made of stuffs thus manufactured he orders to be given to the poor families above described, as they are needed for their winter and their summer dresses. He also has clothing prepared for his armies, and in every city' has a quantity of woollen cloth woven which is paid for from the mount of the tenths levied at the place.

CHAPTER 32

OF THE MANY PERSONS WHO APPLY FOR RELIEF AT THE EMPEROR'S COURT

It should be known that the Tartars, when they followed their original customs, and had not yet adopted the religion of the idolaters, were not in the practice of bestowing alms, and when a poor man applied to them, they drove him away saying, "Begone with your complaint of a bad season which God has sent you; had He loved you, as He loves me, He would have provided for you."

But since the wise men of the idolaters, and especially the Bacsis, already mentioned, have represented to his Majesty that providing for the poor is a good work and highly acceptable to their deities, he has relieved their wants in the manner stated, and at his court none are denied food who come to ask it. Not a day passes in which there are not distributed, by the regular officers, twenty thousand vessels of rice, millet, and panicum. By reason of this admirable and astonishing liberality which the Great Khan exercises towards the poor, the people all adore him.

CHAPTER 34

OF THE RELIGION OF THE TARTARS, OF THE OPINIONS THEY HOLD AS TO THE SOUL, AND OF SOME OF THEIR CUSTOMS

As has already been observed, these people are idolaters, and for deities, each person has a tablet fixed up against a high part of the wall of his chamber, upon which is written a name, that serves to denote the high, celestial, and sublime God. To this they pay daily adoration, with incense burning. Lifting up their hands and then striking their faces against the floor three times, they implore from Him the blessings of sound intellect and health of body; but of Him they ask nothing else. Below this, on the floor, they have a statue which they name Natigay, which they consider as the God of all terrestrial things or whatever is produced from the earth. They give him a wife and children, and worship him in a similar manner, burning incense, raising their hands, and bending to the floor. To him they pray for seasonable weather, abundant crops, increase of family, and the like.

They believe the soul to be immortal, after this fashion. Immediately upon the death of a man, it enters into another body, and that accordingly as he has acted virtuously or wickedly during his life, his future state will become, progressively, better or worse. If he be a poor man, and has conducted himself worthily and decently, he will be re-born, in the first instance, from the womb of a gentlewoman, and become, himself, a gentleman; next, from the womb of a lady of rank, and become a nobleman; thus continually ascending in the scale of existence until he be united to the divinity. But if, on the contrary, being the son of a gentleman, he has behaved unworthily, he will, in his next state, be a clown, and at length a dog, continually descending and going down lower and lower.

Their style (of conversation is courteous; they salute each other politely and with cheerful countenance, have an air of good breeding, and eat their food with particular cleanliness. To their parents they show the utmost reverence. Should it happen that a child acts disrespectfully or neglects to assist his parents when necessary, there is a public tribunal, whose especial duty it is to punish with severity this crime of filial ingratitude.

Malefactors guilty of various crimes, who are apprehended and thrown into prison, are executed by strangling. But such as remain for three years, being the time appointed by his Majesty for a general prison release, and are then liberated, have a mark branded upon one of their cheeks, that they may be recognized.

The present Great Khan has prohibited all species of gambling and other modes of cheating, to which the people of this country are addicted more than any others upon earth. As an argument for deterring them from this practice, he said: "I subdued you by the power of my sword, and consequently whatever you possess belongs of right to me: if you gamble, therefore, you are sporting with my property." He does not, however, take anything arbitrarily in virtue of this right.

The order and regularity observed by all ranks of people, when they present themselves before his Majesty, ought not to pass unnoticed. When they approach within half a mile of the place where he happens to be, they show their respect for his exalted character by assuming a humble, placid, and quiet demeanour, insomuch that not the least noise, nor the voice of any person calling out, or even speaking aloud, is heard. Every man of rank carries with him a small vessel, into which he spits, so long as he continues in the hall of audience, no one daring to spit on the floor; and this being done, he replaces the cover, and makes a salutation. They are accustomed likewise to take with them handsome buskins made of white leather and when they reach the court, but before they enter the hall they put on these white buskins, and give those in which they had walked to the care of the servants. This practice is observed that they may not soil the beautiful carpets, which are curiously wrought with silk and gold, and exhibit a variety of colours.

Discussion Questions

1. What, according to Polo, are the Khan's views of Christianity? How does the Mongol ruler explain his reluctance to convert? How do Mongol religious practices differ from Christian ones?

2. How does Polo characterize Kublai Khan as a ruler? Do you think that Polo accurately represented the emperor? How would the Khan compare with his contemporaries in Europe?

Sources

Marco Polo, *The Travels of Marco Polo*, New York: The Modern Library, 2001.

John Larner, *Marco Polo and the Discovery of the World*, New York and London: Yale University Press, 1999.

BOCCACCIO,
THE DECAMERON

During the life of Boccaccio the morality of the medieval world was fast losing ground to a new outlook defined by humanism and secularism. The contemporary of Chaucer and Petrarch, Boccaccio witnessed the chaotic events of the fourteenth century, from the conflict between secularism and the papacy to the transition from feudalism to mercantilism. He also observed the emergence of the bourgeoisie and the increased use of the Italian vernacular among his fellow Florentines. Boccaccio rightly deserves recognition as one of the founders of the Renaissance for his compassionate and frank assessments of these dramatic transformations.

Boccaccio was born in Tuscany in 1313, the illegitimate son of a Florentine merchant. His father soon legally adopted Boccaccio and raised him to follow the family profession. As a teenager, he and his father moved to Naples, where he frequented the royal court. He became disillusioned with a career in trade, and compromised with his father by studying law. At the same time, he immersed himself in poetry and the classics, making use of his connections at court to take advantage of the fine collections housed in the royal library.

Boccaccio and his father returned to Florence in 1340, where over the course of the next decade the city was convulsed by political scandal, economic failures, famine, and finally the plague. Boccaccio embraced Florentine intellectual and political life upon his return, befriending the circle of poets surrounding Petrarch and also serving as a diplomat for the Florentine government. He had composed his first poems while still in Naples, and continued to write, and even undertook a difficult translation of Livy with the encouragement of his peers. The decade closed with the arrival of the plague in 1348, an epidemic to which Florence lost perhaps half of its population. Boccaccio immediately found inspiration in the events surrounding the plague's arrival and commenced writing his most famous work, known as the *Decameron*.

In the *Decameron*, a group of ten young people who have fled the confines of the city in hopes of avoiding the plague relate one hundred stories over the course of ten days. Boccaccio's introduction to their tales serves as one of the most historically accurate and gruesomely detailed depictions of the Black Death, from the physical symptoms to the breakdown in social order that the disease left in its wake. In the passage to follow, Boccaccio chronicles how both individuals and collective institutions responded to the crisis.

THE DECAMERON

Giovanni Boccaccio

Most gracious ladies, knowing that you are all by nature pitiful, I know that in your judgment this work will seem to have a painful and sad origin. For it brings to mind the unhappy recollection of that late dreadful plague, so pernicious to all who saw or heard of it. But I would not have this frighten you from reading further, as though you were to pass through nothing but sighs and tears in your reading. This dreary opening will be like climbing a steep mountain side to a most beautiful and delightful valley, which appears the more pleasant in proportion to the difficulty of the ascent. The end of happiness is pain, and in like manner misery ends in unexpected happiness.

This brief fatigue (I say brief, because it occupies only a few words) is quickly followed by pleasantness and delight, as I promised you above; which, if I had not promised, you would not expect perhaps from this opening. Indeed, if I could have taken you by any other way than this, which I know to be rough, I would gladly have done so; but since I cannot otherwise tell you how the tales you are about to read came to be told, I am forced by necessity to write in this manner.

In the year 1348 after the fruitful incarnation of the Son of God, that most beautiful of Italian cities, noble Florence, was attacked by deadly plague. It started in the East either through the influence of the heavenly bodies or because God's just anger with our wicked deeds sent it as a punishment to mortal men; and in a few years killed an innumerable quantity of people. Ceaselessly passing from place to place, it extended its miserable length over the West. Against this plague all human wisdom and foresight were vain. Orders had been given to cleanse the city of filth, the entry of any sick person was forbidden, much advice was given for keeping healthy; at the same time humble supplications were made to God by pious persons in processions and otherwise. And yet, in the beginning of the spring of the year mentioned, its horrible results began to appear, and in a miraculous manner. The symptoms were not the same as in the East, where a gush of blood from the nose was the plain sign of inevitable death; but it began both in men and women with certain swellings in the groin or under the armpit. They grew to the size of a small apple or an egg, more or less, and were vulgarly called tumours. In a short space of time these tumours spread from the two parts named all over the body. Soon after this the symptoms changed and black or purple spots appeared on the arms or thighs or any other part of the body, sometimes a few large ones, sometimes many little ones. These spots were a certain sign of death, just as the original tumour had been and still remained.

No doctor's advice, no medicine could overcome or alleviate this disease. An enormous number of ignorant men and women set up as doctors in addition to those who were trained. Either the disease was such that no treatment was possible or the doctors were so ignorant that they did not know what caused it~ and consequently could not administer the proper remedy. In any, case very few recovered; most people died within about three days of the appearance of the tumours described above, most of them without any fever or other symptoms.

The violence of this disease was such that the sick communicated it to the healthy who came near them, just as a fire catches anything dry or oily near it. And it even went further. To speak to or go near the sick brought infection and a common death to the living; and moreover, to touch the clothes or anything else the sick had touched or worn gave the disease to the person touching.

What I am about to tell now is a marvelous thing to hear; and if I and others had not seen it with our own eyes I would not dare to write it, however much I was willing to believe and whatever the good faith of the person from whom I heard it. So violent was the malignancy of this plague that it was communicated, not only from one man to another, but from the garments of a sick or dead man to animals of another species, which caught the disease in that way and very quickly died of it. One day among other occasions I saw with my own eyes (as I said just now) the rags left lying in the street of poor man who had died of the plague; two pigs came along and, as their habit is, turned the clothes over with their snouts and then munched at them with the result that they both fell dead almost at once on the rags, as if they had been poisoned.

From these and similar or greater occurrences, such fear and fanciful notions took possession of the living that almost all of them adopted the same cruel policy, which was entirely to avoid the sick and everything belonging to them. By so doing, each one thought he would secure his own safety.

Some thought that moderate living and the avoidance of all superfluity would preserve them from the epidemic. They formed small communities, living entirely separate from everybody else. They shut themselves up in houses where there were no sick, eating the finest food and drinking the best wine very temperately, avoiding all excess, allowing no news or discussion of death and sickness, and passing the time in music and suchlike pleasures. Others thought just the opposite. They thought the sure cure for the plague was to drink and be merry, to go about singing and amusing themselves, satisfying every appetite they could, laughing and jesting at what happened. They put their words into practice, spent day and night going from tavern to tavern, drinking immoderately, or went into other people's houses, doing only those things which pleased them. This they could easily do because everyone felt doomed and had abandoned his property, so that most houses became common property and any stranger who went in made use of them as if he had owned them. And with all this bestial behaviour, they avoided the sick as much as possible.

In this suffering and misery of our city, the authority of human and divine laws almost disappeared, for, like other men, the ministers and the executors(of the laws were all dead or sick or shut up with their families, so that no duties were carried out. Every man was therefore able to do as he pleased.

Many others adopted a course of life midway between the two just described. They did not restrict their victuals so much as the former, nor allow themselves to be drunken and dissolute like the latter, but satisfied their appetites moderately. They did not shut themselves up, but went about, carrying flowers or scented herbs or perfumes in their hands, in the belief that it was an excellent thing to comfort the brain with such odours; for the whole air was infected with the smell of dead bodies, of sick persons and medicines.

Others again held a still more cruel opinion, which they thought would keep them safe. They said that the only medicine against the plaguestricken was to go right away from them. Men and women, convinced of this and caring about nothing but themselves, abandoned their own city, their own houses, their dwellings, their relatives, their property, and went abroad or at least to the country round Florence, as if God's wrath in punishing men s wickedness with this plague would not follow them but strike only those who remained within the walls of the city, or as if they thought nobody in the city would remain alive and that its last hour had come.

Not everyone who adopted any of these various opinions died, nor did all escape. Some when they were still healthy had set the example of avoiding the sick, and, falling ill themselves, died untended.

One citizen avoided another, hardly any neighbour troubled about others, relatives never or hardly ever visited each other. Moreover, such terror was struck into the hearts of men and women by this calamity, that brother abandoned brother, and the uncle his nephew, and the sister her brother, and very often the wife her husband. What is even worse and nearly incredible is that fathers and mothers refused to see and tend their children, as if they had not been theirs.

Thus, a multitude of sick men and women were left without any care except from the charity of friends (but these were few), or the greed of servants, though not many of these could be had even for high wages. Moreover, most of them were coarse-minded men and women, who did little more than bring the sick what they asked for or watch over them when they were dying. And very often these servants lost their lives and their earnings. Since the sick were thus abandoned by neighbours, relatives and friends, while servants were scarce, a habit sprang up which had never been heard of before. Beautiful and noble women, when they fell sick, did not scruple to take a young or old manservant, whoever he might be, and with no sort of shame, expose every part of their bodies to these men as if they had been women, for they were compelled by the necessity of their sickness to do so. This, perhaps, was a cause of looser morals in those women who survived.

In this way many people died who might have been saved if they had been looked after. Owing to the lack of attendants for the sick and the violence of the plague, such a multitude of people in the city died day and night that it was stupefying to hear of, let alone to see. From sheer necessity, then, several ancient customs were quite altered among the survivors.

The custom had been (as we still see it today), that women relatives and neighbours should gather at the house of the deceased, and there lament with the family. At the same time the men would gather at the door with the male neighbours and other citizens. Then came the clergy, few or many according to the dead person's rank; the coffin was placed on the shoulders of his friends and carried with funeral pomp of lighted candles and dirges to the church which the deceased had chosen before dying. But as the fury of the plague increased, this custom wholly or nearly disappeared, and new customs arose. Thus, people died, not only without having a number of women near them but without a single witness. Very few indeed were honoured with the piteous laments and bitter tears of their relatives, who, on the contrary, spent their time in mirth, feasting and jesting. Even the women abandoned womanly pity and adopted this custom for their own safety. Few were they whose bodies were accompanied to church by more than ten or a dozen neighbours. Nor were these grave and honourable citizens but grave-diggers from the lowest of the people who got themselves called sextons, and performed the task for money. They took up the bier and hurried it off, not to the church chosen by the deceased but to the church nearest, preceded by four or six of the clergy with few candles and often none at all. With the aid of the grave-diggers, the clergy huddled the bodies away in any grave they could find, without giving themselves the trouble of a long or solemn burial service.

The plight of the lower and most of the middle classes was even more pitiful to behold. Most of them remained in their houses, either through poverty or in hopes of safety, and fell sick by thousands. Since they received no care and attention, almost all of them died. Many ended their lives in the streets both at night and during the day; and many others who died in their houses were only known to be dead because the neighbours smelled their decaying bodies. Dead bodies filled every corner. Most of them were treated in the same manner by the survivors, who were more concerned to get rid of their rotting bodies than moved by charity towards the dead. With the aid of porters, if they could get them, they carried the bodies out of the houses and laid them at the doors, where every morning quantities of the dead might be seen. They then were laid on biers, or, as these were often lacking, on tables.

Often a single bier carried two or three bodies, and it happened frequently that a husband and wife, two or three brothers, or father and son were taken off on the same bier. It frequently happened that two priests, each carrying a cross, would go out followed by three or four biers carried by porters; and where the priests thought there was one person to bury, there would be six or eight, and often, even more. Nor were these dead honoured by tears and lighted candles and mourners, for things had reached such a pass that people cared no more for dead men than we care for dead goats. Thus it plainly appeared that what the wise had not learned to endure with patience through the few calamities of ordinary life, became a matter of indifference even to the most ignorant people through the greatness of this misfortune.

Such was the multitude of corpses brought to the churches every day and almost every hour that there was not enough consecrated ground to give them burial, especially since they wanted to bury each person in the family grave, according to the old custom. Although the cemeteries were full they were forced to dig huge trenches, where they buried the bodies by hundreds. Here they stowed them away like bales in the hold of a ship and covered them with a little earth, until the whole trench was full.

Not to pry any further into all the details of the miseries which afflicted our city, I shall add that the surrounding country was spared nothing of what befell Florence. The villages on a smaller scale were like the city; in the fields and isolated farms the poor wretched peasants and their families were without doctors and any assistance, and perished in the highways, in their fields and houses, night and day, more like beasts than men. Just as the townsmen became dissolute and indifferent to their work and property, so the peasants, when they saw that death was upon them, entirely neglected the future fruits of their past labours both from the earth and from cattle, and thought only of enjoying what they had. Thus it happened that cows, asses, sheep, goats, pigs, fowls and even dogs, those faithful companions of man, left the farms and wandered at their will through the fields, where the wheat crops stood abandoned, unreaped and ungarnered. Many of these animals seemed endowed with reason, for, after they had pastured all day, they returned to the farms for the night of their own free will, without being driven.

Returning from the country to the city, it may be said that such was the cruelty of Heaven, and perhaps in part of men, that between March and July more than one hundred thousand persons died within the walls of Florence what between the violence of the plague and the abandonment in which the sick were left by the cowardice of the healthy. And before the plague it was not thought that the whole city held so many people.

Oh, what great palaces, how many fair houses and noble dwellings, once filled with attendants and nobles and ladies, were emptied to the meanest servant! How many famous names and vast possessions and renowned estates were left without an heir! How many gallant men and fair ladies and handsome youths, whom Galen, Hippocrates and AEsculapius themselves would have said were in perfect health, at noon dined with their relatives and friends, and at night supped with their ancestors in the next world!

Discussion Questions

1. According to Boccaccio, how did people respond to the outbreak of the plague?

2. What kind of moral judgments of Florentine society do you find implicit in Boccaccio's description of people's responses?

Sources

Giovanni Boccaccio, *The Decameron of Giovanni Boccaccio*, trans. Richard Aldington, Garden City: Garden City Publishing Company, 1930.

Judish Powers Serafini-Sauli, *Giovanni Boccaccio*, Boston: Twayne Publisher, 1982.

CHAPTER 10

Giovanni Pico della Mirandola
On the Dignity of Man

GIOVANNI PICO DELLA MIRANDOLA, *ON THE DIGNITY OF MAN*

Giovanni Pico's brief life and work epitomized the renewed interest in the classics and the emphasis on the abilities of human beings so typical of the Renaissance. Born in 1463 in the family castle, the young nobleman began his studies in earnest in his teens, traveling to universities in Bologna, Ferrara, Padua, Florence, and finally, the university of Paris. When he returned to Italy in 1486, he undertook a massive work, his nine hundred *Conclusions,* which critiqued the work of classical thinkers, Jewish mystics, scholasticism, and the early Christians. The Pope did not share Pico's enthusiasm for scholarly debate, and Pico's work was found heretical. Exiled to France, Pico vigorously defended his faith, only to encounter further problems. His friend and fellow Renaissance thinker Marsilio Ficino provided Pico with the means to continue his work in Florence, where Pico retired to continue his writings. He sought the Pope's pardon shortly before dying in 1494.

Pico's far-ranging interests contributed to his renown as a formidable Renaissance intellect. His library housed works on literature, theology, philosophy, and science in five languages. Noted for his eclectic interests, especially in Hebrew materials but also in Arabic and Aramaic texts, the heart of his learning lay within the Christian, Latin tradition. The young prince sought to reconcile reason and faith rather than to challenge the rationality of faith.

Pico's *On the Dignity of Man* was written to introduce his nine hundred *Conclusions.* The piece also critiqued his friend Marsilio Ficino's *Platonic Philosophy.* In Pico's view, the greatest attribute of humans is the ability to shape their own nature. God may have granted people the means to do so, but by making people responsible, Pico affirms the human capacity for making moral choices. In the following passage, Pico explains his theory of human nature. His theory is based on the foundations of both reason and religion.

ON THE DIGNITY OF MAN

A Speech by Giovanni Pico della Mirandola,
Prince of Concord

Most venerable fathers, I have read in the records of the Arabians that Abdul the Saracen, on being asked what thing on, so to speak, the world's stage, he viewed as most greatly worthy of wonder, answered that he viewed nothing more wonderful than man. And Mercury's, "a great wonder, Asclepius, is man!" agrees with that opinion. On thinking over the reason for these sayings, I was not satisfied by the many assertions made by many men concerning the outstandingness of human nature: that man is the messenger between creatures, familiar with the upper and king of the lower; by the sharpsightedness of the senses, by the hunting-power of reason, and by the light of intelligence, the interpreter of nature; the part in between the standstill of eternity and the flow of time; and, as the Persians say, the bond tying the world together, nay, the nuptial bond; and, according to David, "a little lower than the angels." These reasons are great but not the chief ones, that is, they are not reasons for a lawful claim to the highest wonder as to a prerogative. Why should we not wonder more at the angels themselves and at the very blessed heavenly choirs?

Finally, it seemed to me that I understood why man is the animal that is most happy, and is therefore worthy of all wonder; and lastly, what the state is that is allotted to man in the succession of things, and that is capable of arousing envy not only in the brutes but also in the stars and even in minds beyond the world. It is wonderful and beyond belief. For this is the reason why man is rightly said and thought to be a great marvel and the animal really worthy of wonder. Now hear what it is, fathers; and with kindly ears and for the sake of your humanity, give me your close attention:

Now the highest Father, God the master-builder, had, by the laws of his secret wisdom, fabricated this house, this world which we see, a very superb temple of divinity. He had adorned the super-celestial region with minds. He had animated the celestial globes with eternal souls; he had filled with a diverse throng of animals the cast-off and residual parts of the lower world. But, with the work finished, the

Artisan desired that there be someone to reckon up the reason of such a big work, to love its beauty, and to wonder at its greatness. Accordingly, now that all things had been completed, as Moses and Timaeus testify, He lastly considered creating man. But there was nothing in the archetypes from which He could mold a new sprout, nor anything in His storehouses which He could bestow as a heritage upon a new son, nor was there an empty judiciary seat where this contemplator of the universe could sit. Everything was filled up; all things had been laid out in the highest, the lowest, and the middle orders. But it did not belong to the paternal power to have failed in the final parturition, as though exhausted by childbearing; it did not belong to wisdom, in a case of necessity, to have been tossed back and forth through want of a plan; it did not belong to the loving-kindness which was going to praise divine liberality in others to be forced to condemn itself. Finally, the best of workmen decided that that to which nothing of its very own could be given should be, in composite fashion, whatsoever had belonged individually to each and every thing. Therefore He took up man, a work of indeterminate form; and, placing him at the midpoint of the world, He spoke to him as follows:

"We have given to thee, Adam, no fixed seat, no form of thy very own, no gift peculiarly thine, that thou mayest feel as thine own, have as thine own, possess as thine own the seat, the form, the gifts which thou thyself shalt desire. A limited nature in other creatures is confined within the laws written down by Us. In conformity with thy free judgment, in whose hands I have placed thee, thou art confined by no bounds; and thou wilt fix limits of nature for thyself. I have placed thee at the center of the world, that from there thou mayest more conveniently look around and see whatsoever is in the world. Neither heavenly nor earthly, neither mortal nor immortal have We made thee. Thou, like a judge appointed for being honorable, art the molder and maker of thyself; thou mayest sculpt thyself into whatever shape thou dost prefer. Thou canst grow downward into the lower natures which are brutes. Thou canst again grow upward from thy soul's reason into the higher natures which are divine."

O great liberality of God the Father! O great and wonderful happiness of man! It is given him to have that which he chooses and to be that which he wills. As soon as brutes are born, they bring with them, "from their dam's bag," as Lucilius says, what they are going to possess. Highest spirits have been, either from the beginning or soon after, that which they are going to be throughout everlasting eternity. At man's birth the Father placed in him every sort of seed and sprouts of every kind of life. The seeds that each man cultivates will grow and bear their fruit in him. If he cultivates vegetable seeds, he will become a plant. If the seeds of sensation, he will grow into brute. If rational, he will come out a heavenly animal. If intellectual, he will be an angel, and a son of God. And if he is not contented with the lot of any creature but takes himself up into the center of his own unity, then, made one spirit with God and settled in the solitary darkness of the Father, who is above all things, he will stand ahead of all things. Who does not wonder at this chameleon which we are? Or who at all feels more wonder at anything else whatsoever? It was not unfittingly that Asclepius the Athenian said that man was symbolized by Prometheus in the secret rites, by reason of our nature sloughing its skin and transforming itself; hence metamorphoses were popular among the Jews and the Pythagoreans. For the more secret Hebrew theology at one time reshapes holy Enoch into an angel of divinity, whom they call *malach hashechina,* and at other times reshapes other men into other divinities. According to the Pythagoreans, wicked men are deformed into brutes and, if you believe Empedocles, into plants too. And copying them, Maumeth [Mohammed] often had it on his lips that he who draws back from divine law becomes a brute. And his saying so was reasonable: for it is not the rind which makes the plant, but a dull and non-sentient nature; not the hide which makes a beast of burden, but a brutal and sensual soul; not the spherical body which makes the heavens, but right reason; and not a separateness from the body but a spiritual intelligence which makes an angel. For example, if you see a man given over to his belly and crawling upon the ground, it is a bush not a man that you see. If you see anyone blinded by the illusions of his empty and Calypso-like imagination, seized by the desire of scratching, and delivered over to the senses, it is a brute not a man that you see. If you come upon a philosopher winnowing out all things by right reason, he is a heavenly not an earthly animal. If you come upon a pure contemplator, ignorant of the body, banished to the innermost places of the mind, he is not an earthly, not a heavenly animal; he more superbly is a divinity clothed with human flesh.

Who is there that does not wonder at man? And it is not unreasonable that in the Mosaic and Christian holy writ man is sometimes denoted by the name "all flesh" and at other times by that of "every creature"; and man fashions, fabricates, transforms himself into the shape of all flesh, into the character of every creature. Accordingly, where Evantes the Persian tells of the Chaldaean theology, he writes that man is not any inborn image of himself, but many images coming in from the outside: hence that saying of the Chaldaeans: *enosh hu shinuy vekamah tevaoth baal chayim,* that is, man is an animal of diverse, multiform, and destructible nature.

But why all this? In order for us to understand that, after having been born in this state so that we may be what we will to be, then, since we are held in honor; we ought to take particular care that no one may say against us that we do not know that we are made similar to brutes and mindless beasts of burden. But rather, as Asaph the prophet says: "Ye are all gods, and sons of the most high," unless by abusing the very indulgent liberality of the Father, we make the free choice, which he gave to us, harmful to ourselves instead of helpful toward salvation. Let a certain holy ambition invade the mind, so that we may not be content with mean things but may aspire to the highest things and strive with all our forces to attain them: for if we will to, we can. Let us spurn earthly things; let us struggle toward the heavenly. Let us put in last place whatever is of the world; and let us fly beyond the chambers of the world to the chamber nearest the most lofty divinity. There, as the sacred mysteries reveal, the seraphim, cherubim, and thrones occupy the first places. Ignorant of how to yield to them and unable to endure the second places, let us compete with the angels in dignity and glory. When we have willed it, we shall be not at all below them.

But by what method? or by doing what? Let us see what they are doing, what life they are living. If we too live that life—for we can— we shall equal their lot. The seraph burns with the fire of charity; the cherub shines with the radiance of intelligence; the throne stands in steadfastness of judgment. Hence, if, dedicated to an active life, we undertake the care of lower things with a right weighing of them, we shall be made stead. fast in the fixed firmness of the thrones. If, being tired of actions and meditating on the workman in the work, on the work in the workman, we are busy with the leisure of contemplation, we shall flash on every side with cherubic light. If by charity we, with his devouring fire, burn for the Workman alone, we shall suddenly burst into flame in the likeness of a seraph. Upon the throne, that is, upon the just judge, sits God, the judge of the ages. He flies above the cherub, that is, the contemplator, and warms him, as if by brooding over him. The Spirit of the Lord is borne above the waters—I mean those waters which are above the heavens, the waters which in Job praise the Lord with hymns before daybreak. He who is a seraph, that is, a lover, is in God; and more, God is in him, and God and he are one.

But in what way can anyone either judge or love things which are unknown? Moses loved God whom he saw, and as judge, he administered to the people what he formerly saw as contemplator on the mountain. Therefore with his own light the cherub in the middle makes us ready for the seraphic fire, and at the same time illuminates us for the judgment of the thrones. He is the bond of the first minds, the order of Pallas, the ruler over contemplative philosophy. We must first rival him and embrace him and lay hold of him. Let us make ourselves one with him and be caught up to the heights of love. And let us descend to the duties of action, well instructed and prepared.

But if our life is to be shaped after the model of a cherub's life, it is well worth while to have in readiness and before our eyes what that life is and what sort it is, what actions and what works are theirs. Since we may not attain to this through ourselves, because we are flesh and our wisdom is of the earth, let us go to the ancient fathers who can give us a very substantial and sure faith in these things as things familiar and akin to them. Let us consult the Apostle Paul, the vessel of election, because, when he was lifted up to the third heaven, he saw the armies of the cherubim in action. According to Dionysius' interpretation, he will answer that the cherubim are being purged, then are being illuminated, and lastly are being perfected. Therefore, by rivaling the life of a cherub upon the earth, by confining the onslaughts of the affections by means of moral science, and by shaking off the mist of reason by means of dialectic, as if washing off the filth of ignorance and vice, let us purge the soul, that the affections may not audaciously run riot, nor an imprudent reason sometime rave. Then, over a soul which has been set in order and purified, let us pour the light of natural philosophy, that lastly we may perfect it with the knowledge of divine things.

Discussion Questions

1. Why does Pico consider humankind a marvel, worthy of wonder?

2. How does Pico use different religious traditions to bolster his views of human nature? How does reason play into his views?

Source

Giovanni Pico della Mirandola, *On the Dignity of Man*, trans. Charles Glenn Wallis with an introduction by Paul J.W. Miller, from *Selections*, Indianopolis and Cambridge: Hackett Publishing Company, Inc., 1998.

CHAPTER 11

Erasmus

The Handbook of the Militant Christian

Jacob Sprenger and Heinrich Kramer

Malleus Maleficarum

ERASMUS, *THE HANDBOOK OF THE MILITANT CHRISTIAN*

Desiderius Erasmus, known as the Prince of the Humanists" was born in the late 1460s in Holland, the illegitimate son of a priest. He lost his parents to the plague in his youth, and those charged with his care encouraged him to join a monastery. The reluctant young man took his vows among the Augustinians in 1492, and a few years later, his superiors sent him to study in Paris. The horrors of living at one of the colleges prompted him to strike out on his own. His success as a private tutor allowed him to support himself. His devotion to teaching lasted throughout his life. While in Paris, he wrote several popular manuals of teaching materials and dared to propose several theories of education, which were also published.

By 1517, Erasmus had decided to not return to his monastery, and sought a dispensation from the pope to continue his religious pursuits as a secular priest

The pope's assent permitted Erasmus to then live as a traveling scholar. His residences in France, Italy, and England led to friendships with some of the greatest thinkers of the time, including Thomas More, with whom he struck up a long-lasting friendship.

Although the university atmosphere had not appealed to him, Erasmus continued his studies independently. He applied his self-acquired knowledge of Greek to write a new a translation of the bible that was published in 1516. Although conservatives and theologians disliked it, the translation paved the way for his international fame. Prince Charles (soon to be Charles V) granted him an appointment at the court, while admirers traveled from near and far to render him homage. Erasmus' moment of glory did not last, however. Erasmus soon provoked the ire of more than theologians. He had initially encouraged Luther's initiatives to reform the church, but soon withdrew that support as the Reformation gathered

momentum and threatened the very survival of the church. Both sides in
the conflict viewed his equivocation with dismay. Erasmus died in 1536,
vilified by Catholics and Protestants alike.

Erasmus constantly advocated a humanist approach to Christianity.
His translation of the bible was one such attempt, as were his efforts to
reform the church's corrupt practices. In 1501, Erasmus drafted *The
Handbook of the Militant Christian,* a manual of Christian habits and
morals. Although the book was commissioned privately, it soon became
tremendously popular throughout Europe. Erasmus proposed a series of
rules that the conscientious Christian should follow. The fifth rule, printed
below, urged the reader to renounce visible, worldly matters for invisible
yet divine ones. The relationship between the divine and the individual is
direct, without relying upon the mediation of a priest or the rituals of the
church.

THE HANDBOOK
OF THE MILITANT CHRISTIAN

Erasmus

FIFTH RULE

Let us add a fifth rule, as a kind of reinforcement to the previous one, that you establish firmly in your mind that perfect piety is the attempt to progress always from visible things, which are usually imperfect or indifferent, to invisible, according to the division of man discussed earlier. This precept is most pertinent to our discussion since it is through neglect or ignorance of it that most Christians are superstitious rather than pious, and except for the name of Christ differ hardly at all from superstitious pagans. Let us imagine, therefore, two worlds, the one merely intelligible, the other visible. The intelligible, which may also be called the angelic, is the one in which God dwells with the blessed spirits, while the visible world comprises the celestial spheres and all that is contained therein. Then there is man, who constitutes, as it were, a third world, participating in the other two, in the visible world through the body, and in the invisible through the soul. Since we are but pilgrims in the visible world, we should never make it our fixed abode, but should relate by a fitting comparison everything that occurs to the senses either to the angelic world or, in more practical terms, to morals and to that part of man that corresponds to the angelic. What the visible sun is here in the visible world the divine mind is in the intelligible world and in that part of you related to it, namely, the spirit. What the moon is here is in that world the assembly of angels and blessed spirits, which they call the church triumphant, and in you it is the spirit. Whatever influence the upper world has over the earth, which lies beneath it, God exercises this same influence over your soul. The sun sets, rises, scorches, becomes temperate, quickens, produces, ripens, attracts, debilitates, cleanses, hardens, softens, illumines, brightens, gladdens. Therefore whatever you observe in it, or rather, whatever you observe in this material world, which is made up of elements, and which some have distinguished from the rest of the universe, and, lastly, whatever you see in the more material part of yourself, learn to refer to God and to the invisible part of yourself. In that way, whatever offers itself to the senses will become for you an occasion for the practice of piety.

As it delights the bodily eye each time this visible sun spreads new light upon the earth, consider for a moment what must be the pleasure of the heavenly spirits, for whom that eternal sun ever rises and never sets; consider what great joy it is for a pure spirit, illumined by divine light. And in response to the promptings of visible creation pray in the words of Paul that 'he who commanded light to shine forth from darkness will begin to shine in your heart to illumine the knowledge of the glory of God in the face of Christ Jesus.' Search out similar passages from the sacred books in which the grace of the divine Spirit is frequently compared to light. Night seems sad and gloomy to you; think of the soul deprived of divine light and shrouded in vice. And if you discern signs of night within yourself, pray that the sun of justice may rise upon you.

Be so convinced of the existence of invisible things that those things that are seen become but mere shadows, which present to the eye only a faint image of invisible realities. Moreover, whatever attracts or repels the senses in material things must be all the more intensely loved or hated by the spirit in the realm of the spirit. A handsome physical appearance is appealing to the eye. Imagine how fair must be the beauty of the soul! A misshapen face is unpleasant to look upon. Consider how odious is a mind deified by vice. And similarly for the rest. For just as the soul has its own comeliness or deformity according as it pleases God or the devil, like rejoicing in like, so it also has a youth of its own, old age, sickness, health, death, life, poverty, riches, pleasure, sorrow, war, peace, cold, heat, thirst, drink, hunger, and food. In a word, whatever we perceive in the body must be understood to exist also in the soul. Therefore the road to the spiritual and perfect life consists in gradually accustoming ourselves to be weaned from those things that do not really exist but appear partly to be what they are not, such as base pleasure or worldly honour, and are partly in a state of flux, hastening to return to nothing, and let ourselves be carried away to things that are real, eternal, unchangeable, and authentic. Socrates, a philosopher not so much in his words as in his life, was aware of this. He said that the soul would migrate happily from the body only if it had previously meditated seriously upon death with the help of philosophy and had long become accustomed to be absent, as it were, from the body through contempt for material things and love and contemplation of spiritual things. The cross to which Christ has called us and the death that Paul wishes us to die together with our Head—echoing the words of the prophet: 'Since for your sake we are slain all the day long and account as sheep for the slaughter,' and expressed by the Apostle in yet other terms: 'Seek the things that are above, not the things that are on earth, have taste for the things that are above'—all of this simply means that we should become numb to material things and render ourselves insensitive to them so that we may have more taste for things that pertain to the spirit as we have less taste for material things. Let us begin to live the interior life all the more sincerely as we live less exteriorly. To sum it all up in simple language, we should be less influenced by transitory things as we come to know more fully the things that are eternal, and we should have less esteem for insubstantial things as we begin to raise our thoughts to those that are real.

Therefore let this rule be ever in readiness, that we do not linger over temporal matters at any time, but move on, rising up to the love of spiritual things, which are incomparably better, despising visible things in comparison to those that are invisible. Illness of the body will be easier to bear if you consider it as a physic of the soul. You will be less solicitous about the health of the body if you concentrate your attention on guarding the health of the soul. Death of the body frightens you, but much more to be dreaded is the death of the soul. You shudder at visible poison, which is deadly to the body, but far more dreadful is the venom that destroys the soul. Hemlock is a poison for the body, but much more deadly is the venom of the soul, sensual pleasures. You are terrified and pale with fear that a lightning bolt, flashing out of the clouds, may strike you, yet how much more to be feared is the invisible lightning bolt of divine wrath: 'Go, ye cursed, into everlasting fire'? You are ravished by physical beauty; why do you show no passion for that beauty which does not manifest itself to the senses? Transfer your love to that beauty which is everlasting, heavenly, and incorruptible, and you will be more moderate in your love of the fleeting and fading beauty of the body. You pray that your field will receive rain, so that it will not dry up; pray rather that God will water your mind so that it will not become unproductive of virtue. With greatest care must you repair the bankruptcy of the soul. You make provisions for your old age so that nothing will be lacking to your body, and should you not take thought that nothing be lacking to the soul?

This is how we should act in the face of all those things that daily present themselves to our senses and variously influence them according to the diversity of their appearance, producing hope, fear, love, hatred, sorrow, and pleasure. . . .

Let what is represented there to the eyes be enacted within you. The death of the Head is represented. Examine yourself in your inmost heart, as they say, to see how close you are to being dead to the world. If you are still subject to anger, ambition, greed, pleasure, and envy, even if you touch the altar, you are still far from the sacrifice. Christ was slain for you; offer these animals to him as sacrificial victims. Sacrifice yourself to him who once immolated himself for you to the Father. If you confide in him without reflecting on these things, God will hate your flabby and gross religion. You were baptized, but do not think that *ipso facto* you became a Christian. Your whole mentality still smacks exclusively of the world; outwardly you are a Christian, but in private you are more pagan than the pagans. Why is that so? Because you possess the body of the sacrament, but you are devoid of its spirit. What does it matter if the body has been washed when the soul remains defiled? What good is it that a few grains of salt have been put on your tongue if the soul remains unsalted? The body has been annointed, but the soul remains unannointed. But if you have been buried with Christ inwardly and are already to walk with him in newness of life, then I recognize you as a Christian. What is the use of being sprinkled with a few drops of holy water as long as you do not wipe clean the inner defilement of the soul? You venerate the saints, and you take pleasure in touching their relics. But you disregard their greatest legacy, the example of a blameless life. No devotion is more pleasing to Mary than the imitation of Mary's humility. No devotion is more acceptable and proper to the saints than striving to imitate their virtues. Would you like to win the favour of Peter and Paul? Imitate the faith of the one and the charity of the other, and you will accomplish more than if you were to dash off to Rome ten times. Would you like to pay the greatest homage to Francis? You are arrogant, you are a worshipper of money, you are quarrelsome. Make this gift to the saint: control your feelings and be more modest after the example of Francis; despise sordid gain and covet the goods of the mind. Abandon you contentiousness and conquer evil with good. That saint will value this honour more than if you were to light a hundred candles before his shrine. Do you think it is important if you are transported to the grave with your head wrapped in the cowl of Francis? Likeness of habit will be of no profit to you when you are dead if your morals were unlike his in life. And although the model of all piety is readily found in Christ, nevertheless, if you take great delight in worshipping Christ in his saints, then make sure you imitate Christ in his saints and in honour of each saint eradicate one vice or strive to attain a particular virtue. If this is the fruit of your devotion, I shall not be averse to these external manifestations.

With great veneration you revere the ashes of Paul, which I do not condemn, if your religion is consistent with your devotion. If you venerate mute and dead ashes and ignore his living image still speaking and breathing, as it were, in his writings, is not your religion utterly absurd? You worship the bones of Paul preserved in a relic casket, but do not worship the mind of Paul hidden away in his writings? You make much of a piece of his body visible through a glass covering, and you do not marvel at the whole mind of Paul shining through his writings? You worship ashes, which are sometimes of some efficacy in removing bodily imperfections; why do you not honour the written word more, by which vices of the soul are healed? Let those without faith to whom these miracles have been accorded express their wonder, but you as a man of faith embrace his writings, so that with the firm belief that God can do all things you may learn to love him above all else. You give homage to an image of Christ's countenance represented in stone or wood or depicted in colour. With how much more religious feeling should you render homage to the image of his mind, which has been reproduced in the Gospels through the artistry of the Holy Spirit. No Apelles has ever portrayed with his brush the shape and features of the body in the way that speech reveals each person's mind and thought. This is especially so with Christ, for as he was the essence of simplicity and truth, there could be no dissimilarity between the archetype of the divine mind and the form of speech that issued from it. Just as nothing is more like the

Father than the Son, the Word of the Father emanating from the innermost recesses of his spirit, so nothing is more like Christ than the word of Christ uttered in the innermost sanctuary of his most holy mind. And you do not gaze with wonder upon this image, do not worship it, scan it with reverent eyes, treasure it in your mind? With such holy and efficacious relics of the Lord at your disposal, do you disregard them and seek out much more extraneous ones? You gaze with awe at what is purported to be the tunic or shroud of Christ, and you read the oracles of Christ apathetically? You think it an immense privilege to have a tiny particle of the cross in your home. But that is nothing compared to carrying about in your heart the mystery of the cross. If such things constitute religion, who could be more religious than the Jews? Even the most impious among them saw Jesus living in the flesh with their own eyes, heard him with their own ears and touched him with their own hands. Who is more fortunate than Judas, who pressed his lips upon the divine mouth? So true is it that the flesh is useless without the spirit that it would have been of no use even to the Virgin Mary to have borne Christ of her own flesh if she had not also conceived his spirit through the Holy Spirit. This is a very great proof, but here is greater still.

As long as the apostles enjoyed the physical company of Christ, do you not read how weak they were and how crass was their understanding? Who could desire anything more to assure his complete salvation than this continuous familiarity between God and man? And yet after the performance of so many miracles, after they had been exposed for so many years to the teaching that proceeded from the mouth of God, after so many proofs of his resurrection, did he not upbraid them for their incredulity at the very last hour as he was about to be received into heaven? What reason can be adduced for this? It was the flesh of Christ that stood in the way, and that is what prompted him to say: 'if I do not go away, the Paraclete will not come. It is expedient for you that I go.' If the physical presence of Christ is of no profit for salvation, shall we dare to place our hopes for the attainment of perfect piety in any material thing? Paul had seen Christ in the flesh. What greater thing can be imagined? But he makes little of that, saying: 'Even if we knew Christ in human terms, we no longer know him in that way.' Why did he not know him? Because he had advanced to a higher state of grace.

Discussion Questions

1. What differentiates the invisible world from the visible? Why is the distinction between the two world crucial for Erasmus?

2. In what ways do the ideas proposed by Erasmus in the fifth rule appear to foreshadow some of the principles of Lutheranism?

Source

Erika Rummel, ed., *The Erasmus Reader*, Toronto, Buffalo and London: University of Toronto Press, 1990.

Jacob Sprenger and Heinrich Kramer, *Malleus Maleficarum*

The famines and plagues of the fourteenth century generated fears of the devil among Europeans. By the end of that century, members of the clergy dreaded another epidemic, although this time the disease attacked the spiritual health of the church's followers. Increasing incidences of witchcraft in the centuries that followed appeared to vindicate their fears and justify the church's extreme response, which took the form of the Inquisition. On the one hand, the outbreak of witchcraft reflected the persistence of pagan customs; on the other, it indicated that the crisis provoked by Luther and Calvin was already latent in the new religious movements blossoming throughout Europe in the late fourteenth century. The struggle with secular rulers had further undermined the authority of the church. In order to consolidate its power in the face of such threats, the papacy issued a bull condemning all manner of heresy in 1484. The pope, Innocent VIII, charged two German inquisitors of the Dominican order, Sprenger and Kramer, with the task of writing a manual elaborating the practical methods by which that bull would be enforced. Sprenger, born in Basel in 1436, had risen quickly through the ranks of the Dominican order and by 1481, held the position of inquisitor for the provinces of Mainz, Trèves, and Cologne. Kramer was likewise an experienced inquisitor.

Their manual, first printed in 1486 under the title *Malleus Maleficarum* or *The Hammer of the Witches,* licensed torture and extermination as the primary means for identifying and suppressing resistance to Christianity. Sprenger and Kramer advised that the dangers posed by the devil and his servants, or witches required these drastic measures. The authors defined a witch as someone, male, but more often female, who had forged a pact with the devil to carry out his evil deeds against Christianity and Christians on earth. *The Malleus* provided a concrete code by which agents of the church could identify witches. The invention of printing enhanced the handbook's popularity. The definitions and remedies proposed by Sprenger and Kramer quickly became the measure of the work of the devil throughout Europe. The German edition sold out repeatedly, and the handbook was also printed in France, Italy, and later, England.

The victims of the Inquisition were largely worshippers of pagan gods, women, and intellectuals or others who questioned the authority of the church. Although the Inquisition had the explicit authorization of the Catholic church, Protestants also persecuted witches after the Reformation. In the passage below, Sprenger and Kramer explain how the devil recruits witches into his brethren, and how other witches in turn enlist new victims.

MALLEUS MALEFICARUM

Jacob Sprenger and Heinrich Kramer

CHAPTER 1

OF THE SEVERAL METHODS BY WHICH DEVILS THROUGH
WITCHES ENTICE AND ALLURE THE INNOCENT TO THE INCREASE
OF THAT HORRID CRAFT AND COMPANY.

THERE are three methods above all by which devils, through the agency of witches, subvert the innocent, and by which that perfidy is continually being increased. And the first is through weariness, through inflicting grievous losses in their temporal possessions. For, as St Gregory says: The devil often tempts us to give way from very weariness. And it is to be understood that it is within the power of a man to resist such temptation; but that God permits it as a warning to us not to give way to sloth. And in this sense is Judges ii to be understood, where it says that God did not destroy those nations, that through them He might prove the people of Israel; and it speaks of the neighbouring nations of the Canaanites, Jebusites, and others. And in our time the Hussites and other Heretics are permitted, so that they cannot be destroyed. Devils, therefore, by means of witches, so afflict their innocent neighbours with temporal losses, that they are as it were compelled, first to beg the suffrages of witches, and at length to submit themselves to their counsels; as many experiences have taught us.

We know a stranger in the diocese of Augsburg, who before he was forty-four years old lost all his horses in succession through witchcraft. His wife, being afflicted with weariness by reason of this, consulted with witches, and after following their counsels, unwholesome as they were, all the horses which he bought after that (for he was a carrier) were preserved from witchcraft.

And how many women have complained to us in our capacity of Inquisitors, that when their cows have been injured by being deprived of their milk, or in any other way, they have consulted with suspected witches, and even been given remedies by them, on condition that they would promise something to some spirit; and when they asked what they would have to promise, the witches answered that it was only a small thing, that they should agree to execute the instructions of that master with regard to certain observances during the Holy Offices of the Church, or to observe some silent reservations in their confessions to priests.

Here it is to be noted that, as has already been hinted, this iniquity has small and scant beginnings, as that at the time of the elevation of the Body of Christ they spit on the ground, or shut their eyes, or mutter some vain words. We know a woman who yet lives, protected by the secular law, who, when the priest at the celebration of the Mass blesses the people, saying, 'Dominus vobiscum', always adds to herself these words in the vulgar tongue, 'Kehr mir die Zung im Arss umb'. Or they even say some such thing at confession after they have received absolution, or do not confess everything, especially mortal sins, and so by slow degrees are led to a total abnegation of the Faith, and to the abominable profession of sacrilege.

This, or something like it, is the method which witches use towards honest matrons who are little given to carnal vices but concerned for worldly profit. But towards young girls, more given to bodily lusts and pleasures, they observe a different method, working through their carnal desires and the pleasures of the flesh.

Here it is to be noted that the devil is more eager and keen to tempt the good than the wicked, although in actual practice he tempts the wicked more than the good, because more aptitude for being tempted is found in the wicked than in the good. Therefore the devil tries all the harder to seduce all the more saintly virgins and girls; and there is reason in this, besides many examples of it.

For since he already possesses the wicked, but not the good, he tries the harder to seduce into his power the good whom he does not, than the wicked whom he does, possess. Similarly any earthly prince takes up arms against those who do not acknowledge his rule rather than against those who do not oppose him.

And here is an example. Two witches were burned in Ratisbon, as we shall tell later where we treat of their methods of raising tempests. And one of them, who was a bath-woman, had confessed among other things the following: that she had suffered much injury from the devil for this reason. There was a certain devout virgin, the daughter of a very rich man whom there is no need to name, since the girl is now dead in the disposition of Divine mercy, and we would not that his thoughts should be perverted by evil; and the witch was ordered to seduce her by inviting her to her house on some Feast Day, in order that the devil himself, in the form of a young man, might speak with her. And although she had tried very often to accomplish this, yet whenever she had spoken to the young girl, she had protected herself with the sign of the Holy Cross. And no one can doubt that she did this at the instigation of a holy Angel, to repel the works of the devil.

Another virgin living in the diocese of Strasburg confessed to one of us that she was alone on a certain Sunday in her father's house, when an old woman of that town came to visit her and, among other scurrilous words, made the following proposition: that, if she liked, she would take her to a place where there were some young men unknown to all the townsmen. And when, said the virgin, I consented, and followed her to her house, the old woman said, 'See, we go upstairs to an upper room where the young men are; but take care not to make the sign of the Cross'. I gave my promise not to do so, and as she was going before me and I was going up the stairs, I secretly crossed myself. At the top of the stairs, when we were both standing outside the room, the hag turned angrily upon me with a horrible countenance, and looking at me said, 'Curse you! Why did you cross yourself? Go away from here. Depart in the name of the devil'. And so I returned unharmed to my home.

It can be seen from this how craftily that old enemy labours in the seduction of souls. For it was in this way that the bath-woman whom we have mentioned, and who was burned, confessed that she had been seduced by some old woman. A different method, however, was used in the case of her companion witch, who had met the devil in human form on the road while she herself was going to visit her lover for the purpose of fornication. And when the Incubus devil had seen her, and had asked her whether she recognized him, and she had said that she did not, he had answered: 'I am the devil; and if you wish, I will always be ready at your pleasure, and will not fail you in any necessity'. And when she had consented, she continued for eighteen years, up to the end of her life, to practise diabolical filthiness with him, together with a total abnegation of the Faith as a necessary condition.

There is also a third method of temptation through the way of sadness and poverty. For when girls have been corrupted, and have been scorned by their lovers after they have immodestly copulated with them in the hope and promise of marriage with them, and have found themselves disappointed in all their hopes and everywhere despised, they turn to the help and protection of devils; either for the sake of vengeance by bewitching those lovers or the wives they have married, or for the sake of giving themselves up to every sort of lechery. Alas! experience tells us that there is no number to such girls, and consequently the witches that spring from this class are in-numerable. Let us give a few out of many examples.

There is a place in the diocese of Brixen where a young man deposed the following facts concerning the bewitchment of his wife.

'In the time of my youth I loved a girl who importuned me to marry her; but I refused her and married another girl from another country. But wishing for friendship's sake to please her, I invited her to the wedding. She came, and while the other honest women were wishing us luck and offering gifts, she raised her hand and, in the hearing of the other women who were standing round, said, 'You will have few days of health after today'. My bride was frightened, since she did not know her (for, as I have said, I had married her from another country), and asked the bystanders who she was who had threatened her in that way; and they said that she was a loose and vagrom woman. None the less, it happened just as she had said. For after a few days my wife was so bewitched that she lost the use of all her limbs, and even now, after ten years, the effects of witchcraft can be seen on her body.'

If we were to collect all the similar instances which have occurred in one town of that diocese, it would take a whole book; but they are written and preserved at the house of the Bishop of Brixen, who still lives to testify to their truth, astounding and unheard-of though they are.

But we must not pass over in silence one unheard-of and astonishing instance. A certain high-born Count in the ward of Westerich, in the diocese of Strasburg, married a noble girl of equal birth; but after he had celebrated the wedding, he was for three years unable to know her carnally, on account, as the event proved, of a certain charm which prevented him. In great anxiety, and not knowing what to do, he called loudly on the Saints of God. It happened that he went to the State of Metz to negotiate some business; and while he was walking about the streets and squares of the city, attended by his servants and domestics, he met a certain woman who had formerly been his mistress. Seeing her, and not at all thinking of the spell that was on him, he spontaneously addressed her kindly for the sake of their old friendship, asking her how she did, and whether she was well. And she, seeing the Count's gentleness, in her turn asked very particularly after his health and affairs; and when he answered that he was well, and that everything prospered with him, she was astonished and was silent for a time. The Count, seeing her thus astonished, again spoke kindly to her, inviting her to converse with him. So she inquired after his wife, and received a similar reply, that she was in all respects well. Then she asked if he had any children; and the Count said he had three sons, one born in each year. At that she was more astonished, and was again silent for a while. And the Count asked her, 'Why, my dear, do you make such careful inquiries? I am sure that you congratulate me on my happiness'. Then she answered, 'Certainly I congratulate you; but curse that old woman who said she would bewitch your body so that you could not have connexion with your wife! And in proof of this, there is a pot in the well in the middle of your yard containing certain objects evilly bewitched, and this was placed there in order that, as long as its contents were preserved intact, for so long you would be unable to cohabit. But see! it is all in vain, and I am glad', etc. On his return home the Count did not delay to have the well drained; and, finding the pot, burned its contents and all, whereupon he immediately recovered the virility which he had lost. Wherefore the Countess again invited all the nobility to a fresh wedding celebration, saying that she was now the Lady of that castle and estate, after having for so long remained a virgin. For the sake of the Count's reputation it is not expedient to name that castle and estate; but we have related this story in order that the truth of the matter may be known, to bring so great a crime into open detestation.

From this it is clear that witches use various methods to increase their numbers. For the above-mentioned woman, because she had been supplanted by the Count's wife, cast that spell upon the Count with the help of another witch; and this is how one witchcraft brings innumerable others in its train.

Discussion Questions

1. What kinds of methods did the devil employ in corrupting the innocent? Why were these practices threatening to the authority of the Church?

2. Why do you think the Inquisition targeted women as practitioners of witchcraft?

Source

Jacob Sprenger and Heinrich Kramer, *Malleus Maleficarum*, trans. Montague Summers, London: Folio Society, 1968.

CHAPTER 12

Bartolomé de Las Casas
The Devastation of the Indies

BARTOLOMÉ DE LAS CASAS, *THE DEVASTATION OF THE INDIES*

Bartolomé de Las Casas, the Dominican priest and onetime Bishop of Chiapas known as the defender of the Indians, began his life in Seville in 1484, the son of a merchant family. He first gained experience in the New World as a soldier in the early 1500s. By all accounts, Las Casas behaved like a typical conquistador, participating in the conquest of Cuba and receiving grants of land and Indian labor from the crown. However, in 1512, he became the first priest ordained in the New World, and in a sermon preached in 1514, Las Casas revealed a change of heart regarding his former activities. He condemned the treatment of the native people by the Spaniards and shortly thereafter, freed his own native slaves. He became a tireless defender of the rights of the indigenous peoples, advocating peaceful conversion, the end of forced labor requirements, and other cruelties imposed upon the conquered peoples. Charles V found Las Casas' arguments compelling, and ruled in favor of more humane treatment, but the new laws were hardly enforceable in the New World.

After years of service, Las Casas was recalled by the Council of the Indies in 1547 to engage in a debate with his leading opponent in the debate over the rights of native peoples. Juan de Sepúlveda and Las Casas stated their positions before an audience of judges, who refused to rule on the matter in the aftermath of the debate. This equivocation demonstrated the complexity of the issue, for although many of the judges sympathized with the arguments of Las Casas, they dared not risk offending important interests in the colonies and Spain.

Las Casas resigned from his bishopric in 1550 to draft and rework a series of polemical manuscripts regarding his experiences in the New World. In 1552, without the permission of the Church, Las Casas published *The Devastation of the Indies,* an account of the conquest and its aftermath exposing the atrocities committed by the conquistadors intended to persuade Charles V to demand further accountability from the conquerors of the New World. Only his reputation protected him from the wrath of the Inquisition. The publication formed the basis for the Black Legend, which portrayed Spain as the agent of needlessly cruel exploitation in the New World and became a useful tool of propaganda against Spain and its empire in the hands of competing European powers. *The Devastation of the Indies* also inaugurated the debate over European contact with indigenous peoples in the New World and the consequences of the interactions between cultures. In the passages below, Las Casas describes the arrival of the Spaniards and the decimation of the native peoples by their conquerors.

THE DEVASTATION OF THE INDIES: A BRIEF ACCOUNT

Bartolomé de Las Casas

THE INDIES were discovered in the year one thousand four hundred and ninety-two. In the following year a great many Spaniards went there with the intention of settling the land. Thus, forty-nine years have passed since the first settlers penetrated the land, the first so-claimed being the large and most happy isle called Hispaniola, which is six hundred leagues in circumference. Around it in all directions are many other islands, some very big, others very small, and all of them were, as we saw with our own eyes, densely populated with native peoples called Indians. This large island was perhaps the most densely populated place in the world. There must be closeto two hundred leagues of land on this island, and the seacoast has been explored for more than ten thousand leagues, and each day more of it is being explored. And all the land so far discovered is a beehive of people; it is as though God had crowded into these lands the great majority of mankind.

And of all the infinite universe of humanity, these people are the most guileless, the most devoid of wickedness and duplicity, the most obedient and faithful to their native masters and to the Spanish Christians whom they serve. They are by nature the most humble, patient, and peaceable, holding no grudges, free from embroilments, neither excitable nor quarrelsome. These people are the most devoid of rancors, hatreds, or desire for vengeance of any people in the world. And because they are so weak and complaisant, they are less able to endure heavy labor and soon die of no matter what malady. The sons of nobles among us, brought up in the enjoyments of life's refinements, are no more delicate than are these Indians, even those among them who are of the lowest rank of laborers. They are also poor people, for they not only possess little but have no desire to possess worldly goods. For this reason they are not arrogant, embittered, or greedy. Their repasts are such that the food of the holy fathers in the desert can scarcely be more parsimonious, scanty, and poor. As to their dress, they are generally naked, with only their pudenda covered somewhat.

And when they cover their shoulders it is with a square cloth no more than two varas in size. They have no beds, but sleep on a kind of matting or else in a kind of suspended net called *hamacas*. They are very clean in their persons, with alert, intelligent minds, docile and open to doctrine, very apt to receive our holy Catholic faith, to be endowed with virtuous customs, and to behave in a godly fashion. And once they begin to hear the tidings of the Faith, they are so insistent on knowing more and on taking the sacraments of the Church and on observing the divine cult that, truly, the missionaries who are here need to be endowed by God with great patience in order to cope with such eagerness. Some of the secular Spaniards who have been here for many years say that the goodness of the Indians is undeniable and that if this gifted people could be brought to know the one true God they would be the most fortunate people in the world.

Yet into this sheepfold, into this land of meek outcasts there came some Spaniards who immediately behaved like ravening wild beasts, wolves, tigers, or lions that had been starved for many days. And Spaniards have behaved in no other way during the past forty years, down to the present time, for they are still acting like ravening beasts, killing, terrorizing, afflicting, torturing, and destroying the native peoples, doing all this with the strangest and most varied new methods of cruelty, never seen or heard of before, and to such a degree that this Island of Hispaniola, once so populous (having a population that I estimated to be more than three millions), has now a population of barely two hundred persons.

The island of Cuba is nearly as long as the distance between Valladolid and Rome; it is now almost completely depopulated. San Juan and Jamaica are two of the largest, most productive and attractive islands; both are now deserted and devastated. On the northern side of Cuba and Hispaniola lie the neighboring Lucayos comprising more than sixty islands including those called Gigantes, beside numerous other islands, some small some large. The least felicitous of them were more fertile and beautiful than the gardens of the King of Seville. They have the healthiest lands in the world, where lived more than five hundred thousand souls; they are now deserted, inhabited by not a single living creature. All the people were slain or died after being taken into captivity and brought to the Island of Hispaniola to be sold as slaves. When the Spaniards saw that some of these had escaped, they sent a ship to find them, and it voyaged for three years among the islands searching for those who had escaped being slaughtered, for a good Christian had helped them escape, taking pity on them and had won them over to Christ; of these there were eleven persons and these I saw.

More than thirty other islands in the vicinity of San Juan are for the most part and for the same reason depopulated, and the land laid waste. On these islands I estimate there are 2,100 leagues of land that have been ruined and depopulated, empty of people.

As for the vast mainland, which is ten times larger than all Spain, even including Aragon and Portugal, containing more land than the distance between Seville and Jerusalem, or more than two thousand leagues, we are sure that our Spaniards, with their cruel and abominable acts, have devastated the land and exterminated the rational people who fully inhabited it. We can estimate very surely and truthfully that in the forty years that have passed, with the infernal actions of the Christians, there have been unjustly slain more than twelve million men, women, and children. In truth, I believe without trying to deceive myself that the number of the slain is more like fifteen million.

The common ways mainly employed by the Spaniards who call themselves Christian and who have gone there to extirpate those pitiful nations and wipe them off the earth is by unjustly waging cruel and bloody wars. Then, when they have slain all those who fought for their lives or to escape the tortures they would have to endure, that is to say, when they have slain all the native rulers and young men (since the Spaniards usually spare only the women and children, who are subjected to the hardest and bitterest servitude ever suffered by man or beast), they enslave any survivors. With these infernal methods of tyranny they debase and weaken countless numbers of those pitiful Indian nations.

Their reason for killing and destroying such an infinite number of souls is that the Christians have an ultimate aim, which is to acquire gold, and to swell themselves with riches in a very brief time and thus rise to a high estate disproportionate to their merits. It should be kept in mind that their insatiable greed and ambition, the greatest ever seen in the world, is the cause of their villainies. And also, those lands are so rich and felicitous, the native peoples so meek and patient, so easy

to subject, that our Spaniards have no more consideration for them
than beasts. And I say this from my own knowledge of the acts I
witnessed. But I should not say "than beasts" for, thanks be to God,
they have treated beasts with some respect; I should say instead like
excrement on the public squares. And thus they have deprived the
Indians of their lives and souls, for the millions I mentioned have died
without the Faith and without the benefit of the sacraments. This is a
well-known and proven fact which even the tyrant Governors,
themselves killers, know and admit. And never have the Indians in all
the Indies committed any act against the Spanish Christians, until those
Christians have first and many times committed countless cruel
aggressions against them or against neighboring nations. For in the
beginning the Indians regarded the Spaniards as angels from Heaven.
Only after the Spaniards had used violence against them, killing,
robbing, torturing, did the Indians ever rise up against them.

HISPANIOLA

On the Island Hispaniola was where the Spaniards first landed, as I
have said. Here those Christians perpetrated their first ravages and
oppressions against the native peoples. This was the first land in the
New World to be destroyed and depopulated by the Christians, and
here they began their subjection of the women and children, taking
them away from the Indians to use them and ill use them, eating the
food they provided with their sweat and toil. The Spaniards did not
content themselves with what the Indians gave them of their own free
will, according to their ability, which was always too little to satisfy
enormous appetites, for a Christian eats and consumes in one day an
amount of food that would suffice to feed three houses inhabited by
ten Indians for one month. And they committed other acts of force and
violence and oppression which made the Indians realize that these men
had not come from Heaven. And some of the Indians concealed their
foods while others concealed their wives and children and still others
fled to the mountains to avoid the terrible transactions of the Christians.

And the Christians attacked them with buffets and beatings, until
finally they laid hands on the nobles of the villages. Then they behaved
with such temerity and shamelessness that the most powerful ruler of
the islands had to see his own wife raped by a Christian officer.

From that time onward the Indians began to seek ways to throw the Christians out of their lands. They took up arms, but their weapons were very weak and of little service in offense and still less in defense. (Because of this, the wars of the Indians against each other are little more than games played by children.) And the Christians, with their horses and swords and pikes began to carry out massacres and strange cruelties against them. They attacked the towns and spared neither the children nor the aged nor pregnant women nor women in childbed, not only stabbing them and dismembering them but cutting them to pieces as if dealing with sheep in the slaughter house. They laid bets as to who, with one stroke of the sword, could split a man in two or could cut off his head or spill out his entrails with a single stroke of the pike. They took infants from their mothers' breasts, snatching them by the legs and, pitching them headfirst against the crags or snatched them by the arms and threw them into the rivers, roaring with laughter and saying as the babies fell into the water, "Boil there, you offspring of the devil!" Other infants they put to the sword along with their mothers and anyone else who happened to be nearby. They made some low wide gallows on which the hanged victim's feet almost touched the ground, stringing up their victims in lots of thirteen, in memory of Our Redeemer and His twelve Apostles, then set burning wood at their feet and thus burned them alive. To others they attached straw or wrapped their whole bodies in straw and set them afire. With still others, all those they wanted to capture alive, they cut off their hands and hung them round the victim's neck, saying, "Go now, carry the message," meaning, Take the news to the Indians who have fled to the mountains. They usually dealt with the chieftains and nobles in the following way: they made a grid of rods which they placed on forked sticks, then lashed the victims to the grid and lighted a smoldering fire underneath, so that little by little, as those captives screamed in despair and torment, their souls would leave them.

I once saw this, when there were four or five nobles lashed on grids and burning; I seem even to recall that there were two or three pairs of grids where others were burning, and because they uttered such loud screams that they disturbed the captain's sleep, he ordered them to be strangled. And the constable, who was worse than an executioner, did not want to obey that order (and I know the name of that constable and know his relatives in Seville), but instead put a stick over the victims' tongues, so they could not make a sound, and he stirred up the fire, but not too much, so that they roasted slowly, as he liked. I saw all these things I have described, and countless others.

And because all the people who could do so fled to the mountains to escape these inhuman, ruthless, and ferocious acts, the Spanish captains, enemies of the human race, pursued them with the fierce dogs they kept which attacked the Indians, tearing them to pieces and devouring them. And because on few and far between occasions, the Indians justifiably killed some Christians, the Spaniards made a rule among themselves that for every Christian slain by the Indians, they would slay a hundred Indians.

Discussion Questions

1. How does Las Casas portray the conquistadors? How are the Indians portrayed in comparison?

2. How convincing are Las Casas' accusations of devastation and genocide? Do you think his representation of the events of the conquest ring historically true?

Source

Bartolomé de las Casas, *The Devastation of the Indies: A Brief Account*, trans. Herma Briffault, Baltimore and London: The Johns Hopkins University Press, 1992.

CHAPTER 13

Madame de Lafayette
The Princess of Clèves

John Locke
Second Treatise of Government

Madame de Lafayette, *The Princess of Clèves*

The Countess of Lafayette, born Marie Madeleine Pioche de La Vergne, grew up on the outskirts of Paris. As a teenager she waited upon the Queen for a number of years, learning firsthand about the intrigues of the royal court. She married rather late for a woman of her class. The Count of Lafayette, a provincial nobleman, was a man twice her twenty-one years, but nonetheless a desirable match for a woman from a modest family. Their relationship may have lacked passion, but the Countess assumed control of her husband's business interests in Paris with enthusiasm. She remained happily in the city, while the Count pursued his interests at his castle in Auvergne. In Paris, she remained abreast of the developments at the court, and enjoyed the company of several notable writers and intellectuals, who admired her for her wit and reason.

The primary concerns of the courtiers in the mid to late seventeenth century revolved around love. Madame de Lafayette understood, in keeping with her times, that love and marriage were hardly reconcilable, yet love often led to tragic outcomes. *The Princess of Clèves* was first published anonymously in 1678 in four parts because Madame de La Fayette feared the novel might reflect poorly upon her reputation by implying that she herself had indulged in amorous indiscretions. The tale of a love affair between a married woman, Madame de Clèves, and the Duke of Nemours at the court of Henry II, the novel reflects more accurately the social milieu surrounding Louis XIV than the historical moment it purports to depict.

The book immediately created an outcry among Parisians for its unflinching portrayal of the duplicity and frivolity of courtly society. In the passage below, the mother of the Princess, reproaches her married daughter's suitor, the Duke of Nemours, by regaling him with a tale of the royal family's disastrous romantic liaisons. The Duke shows little patience with these reproaches, while the daughter, Madame de Clèves does not sense the dangers that such an affair might involve for her.

THE PRINCESS OF CLÈVES

Madame de Lafayette

"If you judge by appearances in this place," replied Madame de
Chartres, "you will often be deceived; what appears on the surface is
almost never the truth". But to return to Madame de Valentinois—you
know that she is called 'Diana of Poitiers.' Her family is very illustrious;
it issues from the ancient Dukes of Aquitaine; her grandmother was an
illegitimate daughter of Louis XI, and, in short, there is nothing but
greatness in her ancestry. Saint-Valier, her father, was mixed up in the
affair of the Connétable de Bourbon, of which you have heard. He was
condemned to death and taken to the scaffold. His daughter, whose
beauty was wonderful and who had already attracted the late King, did
so well (I know not what means she employed) that she saved her
father's life. The pardon arrived when he was awaiting the death-blow;
but fear had so seized upon him that he had lost consciousness, and
died a few days later. His daughter appeared at Court as the King's
Mistress. The journey to Italy and the King's imprisonment interrupted
this love-affair. When he came back from Spain and the Queen Regent
went to meet him at Bayonne, she took with her all her maids-of-
honour, among whom was Mademoiselle de Pisseleu, who later
became Duchess of Étampes. The King fell in love with her. She was
inferior in birth, intelligence, and beauty to Madame de Valentinois, and
she had only one advantage over the latter—that of extreme youth. I
have heard her say several times that she was born the day Diana of
Poitiers was married. There was more hatred than truth in this
statement, for I am sorely mistaken if the Duchess of Valentinois did
not marry Monsieur de Brézé, Grand Seneschal of Normandy, at the
time when the King fell in love with Madame d'Étampes. Never was
there such hatred as that between these two women. The Duchess of
Valentinois could not forgive Madame d'Étampes for having deprived
her of the title of the King's Mistress. Madame d'Étampes cherished
violent jealousy against Madame de Valentinois because the King had
not severed his relations with her. This Prince was not scrupulously
faithful to his mistresses. There was always one who enjoyed the title
and the honours, but the ladies known as the 'little band' shared him in

turns. The loss of his son the Dauphin, who died at Tournon and who was believed to have been poisoned, caused him deep grief. He had neither the same tenderness for his second son, who now reigns, nor the same appreciation of his qualities: he considered that he was not bold or vivacious enough. He complained of this one day to Madame de Valentinois, and she told him that she would have him fall in love with her, to make him more lively and more agreeable. She succeeded, as you see. The love has lasted for more than twenty years, without being diminished by time or obstacle.

"The late King was at first opposed to it; and, either because he still loved Madame de Valentinois enough to be jealous or because he was urged on by the Duchess of Étampes, who was in despair at the Dauphin's attachment to her enemy, it is certain that this love affair caused him anger and chagrin, of which he gave daily evidence. His son feared neither his anger nor his hatred, and nothing could force him to lessen or hide his love: the King had to get used to it. This opposition to his wishes estranged him still more from the Dauphin, and attached him more to the Duke of Orleans, his third son. He was a comely, handsome Prince, full of ardour and ambition, with an irrepressible youth which needed moderating, but he would have become a very distinguished Prince if age had ripened his judgment.

"The Dauphin's rank as heir and the King's favour for the Duke of Orleans caused between the two Princes a sort of emulation that was pushed to hatred. This emulation began in childhood, and had always continued. When the Emperor passed through France, he gave his whole preference to the Duke of Orleans rather than to the Dauphin, who felt it so keenly that, when the Emperor was at Chantilly, he wished to force the Connétable to arrest him without waiting for the King's orders. The Connétable would not do so. The King blamed him afterwards for not having carried out his son's decision; and, when he banished the Connétable from Court, this reason had much to do with it.

"The estrangement of the two brothers gave the Duchess of Étampes the idea of enlisting the aid of the Duke of Orleans to support her in the King's favour and to thwart the Duchess of Valentinois. She succeeded in this. The Prince, though not in love with her, supported her interests almost as warmly as the Dauphin did those of Madame de Valentinois. That made two cliques at Court, as you may well imagine. And these intrigues did not stop at women's quarrels.

"The Emperor, who had retained his feeling of friendship for the Duke of Orleans, had offered several times to cede to him the Duchy of Milan. In the proposals of peace made later, he held out the hope of giving him the Seventeen Provinces, and of having him marry his daughter. The Dauphin was anxious neither for the peace nor for the marriage. He made use of the Connétable, whom he has always loved, to point out to the King the importance of not making his successor's brother as powerful as a Duke of Orleans would be if he had the support of the Emperor and of the Seventeen Provinces. The Connétable was all the more of the Dauphin's opinion because he thus opposed the desires of Madame d'Étampes, who was his bitter enemy and who ardently desired the advancement of the Duke of Orleans.

"The Dauphin, at the time, was commanding the King's forces in Champagne, and had reduced those of the Emperor to such an extremity that they would have entirely perished if the Duchess of Étampes, fearing that too great a success would make us refuse peace and the alliance of the Emperor with the Duke of Orleans, had not secretly told the enemy to surprise Épernay and Châtaeau Thierry, which were full of victuals. They did this, and, in this way, saved all their army.

"The Duchess did not long enjoy the success of her treachery. Shortly afterwards, the Duke of Orleans died at Farmoutiers, of some kind of contagious disease. He loved one of the most beautiful women at Court, and was loved by her. I shall not name her, because she had since lived so virtuously, and because she hid with such care her love for the Prince, that her reputation deserves to be respected. Fate willed that she should hear of her husband's death on the very day she learned of the death of the Duke of Orleans, so that she was able to hide the real cause of her affliction without having to restrain her grief.

"The King did not long survive his son: he died two years later. He recommended the Dauphin to make use of Cardinal de Tournon and Admiral d'Annebault, and he did not mention the Connétable, who was at that time exiled at Chantilly. Yet the first thing the new King did was to recall him and give him charge of affairs.

"Madame d'Étampes was sent away, and received all the ill-treatment that she could expect from an all-powerful enemy. The Duchess of Valentinois avenged herself to the full on her rival and on all those who had thwarted her. Her power over the King's mind appeared to be even more absolute than it had appeared to be while he was still Dauphin. During the twelve years the King has reigned, she has been absolute mistress over all. She disposes of offices and of affairs of State; she has had dismissed Cardinal de Tournon, Chancellor Olivier and Villeroy.

"Those who wished to enlighten the King as to her conduct have perished in the attempt. Count de Taix, Grand Master of Artillery, who did not like her, could not refrain from speaking of her love-affairs, especially that with Count de Brissac, of whom the King had already been very jealous. Nevertheless, she played her cards so well that Count de Taix was disgraced: his command was taken from him and—which is almost unbelievable—she had it given to Count de Brissac. Later, she made him Marshal of France.

"The King's jealousy increased, however, to such a degree that he could not suffer the Marshal's remaining at Court. But jealousy, harsh and violent in all others, was gentle and moderate in him, because of the extreme respect that he had for his Mistress; so that he did not dare send his rival away, except on the pretext of giving him the Governorship of Piedmont. Brissac passed many years there; he came back last winter, ostensibly to ask for troops and for other things necessary for the army he commanded. The wish to see Madame de Valentinois and the fear of being forgotten by her had perhaps more to do with his journey.

"The King received him very coldly. The Guises, who did not like him, but did not dare show their feelings because of Madame de Valentinois, used the Vidame, who was his avowed enemy, to prevent his obtaining any of the things he came to seek. It was not hard to thwart him: the King hated him, and his presence caused him uneasiness, so that he was forced to go back without any fruit of his journey except perhaps the strengthening in Madame de Valentinois of feelings that absence was beginning to weaken. The King had had many other grounds for jealousy, but he did not know of them or he did not dare to complain.

"I do not know, daughter," added Madame de Chartres, "whether you do not think that I have told you of more things than you wished to hear."

"I am very far, Madame, from thus complaining," replied Madame de Clèves, "and, were it not that I fear to be importunate, I should ask you further of many circumstances of which I am ignorant."

Monsieur de Nemours' love for Madame de Clèves was from the first so violent that it deprived him of the taste for, even of the memory of, all the ladies he had loved and with whom he had kept up correspondence during his absence. He did not even take the trouble to seek excuses for breaking with them: he had no patience to listen to their complaints or reply to their reproaches. The Dauphiness, for whom he had had a somewhat strong passion, could not occupy his heart in competition with Madame de Clèves. Even his impatience to go to England began to abate, and he did not urge with as much ardour as before the arrangements necessary for his departure. He often went to the Dauphiness' because Madame de Clèves was often there, and he was not averse to having people imagine what had been believed concerning his feelings for the Queen in question. Madame de Clèves seemed to him so precious that he decided to refrain from giving her any indication of his love rather than risk having the public know of it. He did not speak of it even to the Vidame de Chartres, who was his close friend and from whom he hid nothing. He ordered his life so wisely, and was so careful, that no one save the Chevalier de Guise suspected him of being in love with Madame de Clèves; and she herself would have found it difficult to perceive if the inclination she had for him had not caused her closely to observe his actions, which left no doubt in her mind.

She did not feel as ready to tell her mother what she thought of the feelings of this Prince as she had been to speak to her concerning her other suitors; without any deliberate intention of hiding the matter from her, she did not speak about it. But Madame de Chartres saw it only too clearly, as well as the inclination that her daughter had for him. This knowledge caused her real pain: she saw clearly the peril of this young girl, loved by a man as attractive as Monsieur de Nemours and feeling some inclination for him. Her suspicions of this inclination were completely confirmed by something that happened a few days later.

Marshal de Saint-André, who sought every occasion to show his magnificence, earnestly begged the King, on the pretext of showing him his house, the building of which was just finished, to do him the honour of supping there with the Queens. The Marshal was also very pleased to display before Madame de Clèves a lavish expenditure that did not fall short of profusion.

Some days before the date chosen for the supper, the Dauphin, whose health was rather bad, had fallen ill and had received no visitors. The Queen, his wife, had spent the whole day with him.

Madame de Clèves did not appear to be listening to what the Prince of Condé was saying, but she was paying careful attention to every word. She easily guessed the share she had in the cause upheld by Monsieur de Nemours, and especially in what he said of the suffering caused by not being at a ball attended by the loved one, for he was not to be at Marshal de Saint-André's ball, as the King had charged him to go and meet the Duke of Ferrara.

The Dauphiness laughed with the Prince of Condé, and did not agree with the opinion of Monsieur de Nemours.

"There is only one occasion," said the Prince, "on which Monsieur de Nemours agrees that the lady he loves may go to a ball: it is when he gives it himself. He admits that last year, when he gave one for Your Majesty, he considered that his lady-love conferred a favour on him by coming, although she seemed to be merely attending you. He thinks it is always conferring a favour on a lover to take part in a pleasure offered by him—that it is always pleasant for a lover to have his lady see him master of a place in which all the Court assembles, and successfully doing the honours."

"Monsieur de Nemours was right," said the Dauphiness, with a smile, "to approve of his lady-love's going to the ball; there were at that time so many ladies to whom he gave the title that, had they not been present, there would have been few people there."

Discussion Questions

1. What morals can be drawn from Madame de Chartres' story about Madame de Valentinois?
2. Why did a love affair hold so much risk for Madame de Clèves? Did men and women face unequal hazards when engaging in extramarital relations?

Sources

Madame de La Fayette, *The Princess of Clèves*, trans H. Ashton, London: The Nonesuch Press, 1943.

Stirling Haig, *Madame de Lafayette*, New York: Twayne Publishers, 1970.

JOHN LOCKE, *SECOND TREATISE OF GOVERNMENT*

John Locke was born in 1632 to a family of modest means in Somerset. His father had fought in the Parliamentary army during the English civil war of the 1640s, and his family leaned toward Puritanism. He was educated at some of the finest English schools, and became a graduate fellow and teacher at Christ Church, Oxford in his 20s and early 30s, where he taught philosophy and studied medicine. He maintained an uneasy relationship with the Oxford colleges, whose deans disapproved of some of his early writings. Locke remained at the institution until 1665, and after a brief stint as a diplomat, joined the household of Anthony Ashley Cooper, the Earl of Shaftesbury.

Upon becoming the physician of the Earl of Shaftesbury, Locke entered into a world of political intrigue. His presence in the Shaftesbury household owed as much to their shared political leanings as it did to Locke's medical knowledge. The Earl, once a supporter of Charles II, had opposed Charles' increasingly absolutist measures and the imminent succession of the Catholic James II. Charles II reacted by dissolving Parliament, and Earl and his following were persecuted. Locke likely drafted the *Second Treatise of Government* sometime between 1679 and 1683 with the encouragement of the Earl of Shaftesbury, just as these events were taking shape. However, circumstances forced Locke to flee to Holland in 1683, where he remained until 1689 when the victory of William and Mary over James and the passing of a Bill of Rights in 1689 guaranteed his safe return.

His *Second Treatise* was not published until 1690, serving to explain the Glorious Revolution after the fact rather than to justify it, as the piece had been intended. Locke did not acknowledge authorship, fearing repercussions if the political climate again shifted. The publication immediately became an enduring classic in political theory. Locke's notions of limited government and the right to rebel inspired revolutionaries over the course of the next century, and his work remains popular because of his ideas regarding the inseparability of property rights, individual liberties, and a liberal constitutional state. In the sections below, Locke explains the advantages of government for individuals. Then he defines his conception of a commonwealth before exploring the limits of the legislative powers of within a commonwealth.

SECOND TREATISE OF GOVERNMENT

John Locke

CHAP. IX.

OF THE ENDS OF POLITICAL SOCIETY AND GOVERNMENT.

§. 123. IF man in the state of nature be so free, as has been said; if he be absolute lord of his own person and possessions, equal to the greatest, and subject to no body, why will he part with his freedom? why will he give up this empire, and subject himself to the dominion and controul of any other power? To which it is obvious to answer, that though in the state of nature he hath such a right, yet the enjoyment of it is very uncertain, and constantly exposed to the invasion of others: for all being kings as as he, every man his equal, and the greater part no strict observers of equity and justice, the enjoyment of the property he has in this state is very unsafe, very unsecure. This makes him willing to quit a condition, which, however free, is full of fears and continual dangers: and it is not without reason, that he seeks out, and is willing to join in society with others, who are already united, or have a mind to unite, for the mutual *preservation* of their lives, liberties and estates, which I call by the general name, *property*.

§.124. The great and *chief end*, therefore, of men's uniting into common-wealths, and putting themselves under government, *is the preservation of their property*. To which in the state of nature there are many things wanting.

First, There wants an *established*, settled, known *law*, received and allowed by common consent to be the standard of right and wrong, and the common measure to decide all controversies between them: for though the law of nature be plain and intelligible to all rational creatures; yet men being biassed by their interest, as well as ignorant for want of study of it, are not apt to allow of it as a law binding to them in the application of it to their particular cases.

§. 125. *Secondly*, In the state of nature there wants *a known and indifferent judge*, with authority to determine all differences according to the established law: for every one in that state being both judge and executioner of the law of nature, men being partial to themselves, passion and revenge is very apt to carry them too far, and with too much heat, in their own cases; as well as negligence, and unconcernedness, to make them too remiss in other men's.

§. 126. *Thirdly,* In the state of nature there often wants *power* to back and support the sentence when right, and to *give* it due *execution.* They who by any injustice offended, will seldom fail, where they are able, by force to make good their injustice; such resistance many times makes the punishment dangerous, and frequently destructive, to those who attempt it.

§. 127. Thus mankind, notwithstanding all the privileges of the state of nature, being but in an ill condition, while they remain in it, are quickly driven into society. Hence it comes to pass, that we seldom find any number of men live any time together in this state. The inconveniencies that they are therein exposed to, by the irregular and uncertain exercise of the power every man has of punishing the transgressions of others, make them take sanctuary under the established laws of government, and therein seek *the preservation of their property.* It is this makes them so willingly give up every one his single power of punishing, to be exercised by such alone, as shall be appointed to it amongst them; and by such rules as the community, or those authorized by them to that purpose, shall agree on. And in this we have the original *right and rise of both the legislative and executive power,* as well as of the governments and societies themselves.

§. 128. For in the state of nature, to omit the liberty he has of innocent delights, a man has two powers.

The first is to do whatsoever he thinks fit for the preservation of himself, and others within the permission of the *law of nature:* by which law, common to them all, he and all the rest of *mankind are one community,* make up one society, distinct from all other creatures. And were it not for the corruption and vitiousness of degenerate men, there would be no need of any other; no necessity that men should separate from this great and natural community, and by positive agreements combine into smaller and divided associations.

The other power a man has in the state of nature, is the *power to punish the crimes* committed against that law. Both these he gives up, when he joins in a private, if I may call it so, or particular politic society, and incorporates into any common-wealth, separate from the rest of mankind.

§. 129. The first *power*, viz. *of doing whatsoever he thought for the preservation of himself*, and the rest of mankind, *he gives up* to be regulated by laws made by the society, so far forth as the preservation of himself, and the rest of that society shall require; which laws of the society in many things confine the liberty he had by the law of nature.

§. 130. *Secondly, The power of punishing he wholly gives up*, and engages his natural force, (which he might before employ in the execution of the law of nature, by his own single authority,as he thought fit) to assist the executive power of the society, as the law thereof shall require: for being now in a new state, wherein he is to enjoy many conveniencies, from the labour, assistance, and society of others in the same community, as well as protection from its whole strength; he is to part also with as much of his natural liberty, in providing for himself, as the good, prosperity, and safety of the society shall require; which is not only necessary, but just, since the other members of the society do the like.

§ 131. But though men, when they enter into society, give up the equality, liberty, and executive power they had in the state of nature, into the hands of the society to be so far disposed of by the legislative as the good of the society shall require; yet it being only with an intention in every one the better to preserve himself, his liberty and property; (for no rational creature can be supposed to change his condition with an intention to be worse) the power of the society, or *legislative* constituted by them, can *never be supposed to extend farther, than the common good*; but is obliged to secure every one's property, by providing against those three defects above mentioned, that made the state of nature so unsafe and uneasy. And so whoever has the legislative or supreme power of any common-wealth, is bound to govern by established *standing laws*, promulgated and known to the people, and not by extemporary decrees; by *indifferent* upright *judges*, who are to decide controversies by those laws; and to employ the force of the community at home, *only in the execution of such laws*, or abroad to prevent or redress foreign injuries, and secure the community from inroads and invasion. And all this to be directed to no other *end*, but the *peace, safety*, and *public good* of the people.

CHAP. X.

OF THE FORMS OF A COMMON-WEALTH.

§. 132. THE majority having, as has been shewed, upon men's first uniting into society, the whole power of the community naturally in them, may employ all that power in making laws for the community from time to time, and executing those laws by officers of their own appointing; and then the *form* of the government is a perfect *democracy:* or else may put the power of making laws into the hands of a few select men, and their heirs or successors; and then it is an *oligarchy:* or else into the hands of one man, and then it is a *monarchy:* if to him and his heirs, it is an *hereditary monarchy:* if to him only for life, but upon his death the power only of nominating a successor to return to them; an *elective monarchy.* And so accordingly of these the community may make compounded and mixed forms of government, as they think good. And if the legislative power be at first given by the majority to one or more persons only for their lives, or any limited time, and then the supreme power to revert to them again; when it is so reverted, the community may dispose of it again anew into what hands they please, and so constitute a new form of government: for the *form of government depending upon the placing the* supreme power, which is the legislative, it being impossible to conceive that an inferior power should prescribe to a superior, or any but the supreme make laws, according as the power of making laws is placed, such is the *form of the common-wealth.*

§. 133. By *common-wealth,* I must be understood all along to mean, not a democracy, or any form of government, but *any independent community,* which the *Latines* signified by the word *civitas,* to which the word which best answers in our language, is *common-wealth,* and most properly expresses such a society of men, which community or city in *English* does not; for there may be subordinate communities in a government; and city amongst us has a quite different notion from common-wealth: and therefore, to avoid ambiguity, I crave leave to use the word *common-wealth* in that sense, in which I find it used by king *James the first;* and I take it to be its genuine signification; which if any body dislike, I consent with him to change it for a better.

CHAP. XI.

OF THE EXTENT OF THE LEGISLATIVE POWER.

§ 134. THE great end of men's entering into society, being the enjoyment of their properties in peace and safety, and the great instrument and means of that being the laws established in that society; the *first and fundamental positive law* of all common-wealths *is the establishing of the legislative* power; as the *first and fundamental natural law,* which is to govern even the legislative itself, is the *preservation of the society,* and (as far as will consist with the public good) of every person in it. This *legislative* is not only the *supreme power* of the common-wealth, but sacred and unalterable in the hands where the community have once placed it; nor can any edict of any body else, in what form soever conceived, or by what power soever backed, have the force and obligation of a *law,* which has not its *sanction* from that *legislative* which the public has chosen and appointed: for without this the law could not have that, which is absolutely necessary to its being a *law, the consent of the society,* over whom no body can have a power to make laws, but by their own consent, and by authority received from them; and therefore all the *obedience,* which by the most solemn ties any one can be obliged to pay, ultimately terminates in this *supreme power,* and is directed by those laws which it enacts; nor can any oaths to any foreign power whatsoever, or any domestic subordinate power, discharge any member of the society from his *obedience to the legislative,* acting pursuant to their trust; nor oblige him to any obedience contrary to the laws so enacted, or farther than they do allow; it being ridiculous to imagine one can be tied ultimately to *obey* any *power* in the society, which is not the *supreme.*

§. 135. Though the *legislative,* whether placed in one or more, whether it be always in being, or only by intervals, though it be the *supreme* power in every common-wealth; yet,

First, It is *not,* nor can possibly be absolutely *arbitrary* over the lives and fortunes of the people: for it being but the joint power of every member of the society given up to that person, or assembly, which is legislator; it can be no more than those persons had in a state of nature before they entered into society, and gave up to the community: for no body can transfer to another more power than he has in himself; and no body has an absolute arbitrary power over himself, or over any other, to destroy his own life, or take away the life or property of another. A man, as has been proved, cannot subject himself to the arbitrary power of another; and having in the state of nature no arbitrary power over the life, liberty, or possession of another, but only so much as the law of nature gave him for the preservation of himself, and the rest of mankind; this is all he doth, or can give up to the common-wealth, and by it to *the legislative power*, so that the legislative can have no more than this. Their power, in the utmost bounds of it, is *limited to the public good* of the society. It is a power, that hath no other end but preservation and therefore can never have a right to destroy, enslave, or designedly to impoverish the subjects. The obligations of the law of nature cease not in society, but only in many cases are drawn closer, and have by human laws known penalties annexed to them, to inforce their observation. Thus the law of nature stands as an eternal rule to all men, *legislators* as well as others. The *rules* that they make for other men's actions, must, as well as their own and other men's actions, be conformable to the law of nature, *i.e.* to the will of God, of which that is a declaration, and the *fundamental law of nature being the preservation of mankind*, no human sanction can be good, or valid against it.

§. 136. *Secondly,* The *legislative,* or supreme authority, cannot assume to its self a power to rule by extemporary arbitrary decrees, but *is bound to dispense justice,* and decide the rights of the subject *by promulgated standing laws, and known authorized judges:* for the law of nature being unwritten, and so no where to be found but in the minds of men, they who through passion or interest shall miscite, or misapply it, cannot so easily be convinced of their mistake where there is no established judge: and so it serves not, as it ought, to determine the rights, and fence the properties of those that live under it, especially where every one is judge, interpreter, and executioner of it too, and that in his own case: and he that has right on his side, having ordinarily but his own single strength, hath not force enough to defend himself from injuries, or to punish delinquents. To avoid these inconveniences, which disorder men's properties in the state of nature, men unite into societies, that they may have the united strength of the whole to secure and defend their properties, and may have *standing rules* to bound it, by which every one may know what is his. To this end it is that men give up all their natural power to the society which they enter into, and the community put the legislative into the hands as they think fit, with this trust, that they shall be governed by *declared laws,* or else their peace, quiet, and property will still be at the same uncertainty, as it was in the state of nature.

§. 137. Absolute arbitrary power, or governing without *settled standing laws,* can neither of them consist with the ends of society and government, which men would not quit the freedom of the state of nature for, and tie themselves up under, were it not to preserve their lives, liberties and fortunes, and by *stated rules* of right and property to secure their peace and quiet. It cannot be supposed that they should intend, had they a power so to do, to give to any one, or more, an *absolute arbitrary power* over their persons and estates, and put a force into the magistrate's hand to execute his unlimited will arbitrarily upon them. This were to put themselves into a worse condition than the state of nature, wherein they had a liberty to defend their right against the injuries of others, and were upon equal terms of force to maintain it, whether invaded by a single man, or many in combination. Whereas by supposing they have given up themselves to the *absolute arbitrary power* and will of a legislator, they have disarmed themselves, and armed him, to make a prey of them when he pleases; he being in a much worse condition, who is exposed to the arbitrary power of one man, who has the command of 100,000, than he that is exposed to the arbitrary power of 100,000 single men; no body being secure, that his will, who has such a command, is better than that of other men, though his force be 100,000 times stronger. And therefore, whatever form the common-wealth is under, the ruling power ought to govern by *declared* and *received laws,* and not by extemporary dictates and undetermined resolutions: for then mankind will be in far worse condition than in the state of nature, if they shall have armed one, or a few men with the joint power of a multitude, to force them to obey at pleasure the exorbitant and unlimited decrees of their sudden thoughts, or unrestrained, and till that moment unknown wills, without having any measures set down which may guide and justify their actions: for all the power the government has, being only for the good of the society, as it ought not to be *arbitrary* and at pleasure, so it ought to be exercised by *established and promulgated laws;* that both the people may know their duty, and be safe and secure within the limits of the law; and the rulers too kept within their bounds, and not be tempted, by the power they have in their hands, to employ it to such purposes, and by such measures, as they would not have known, and own not willingly.

§. 138. *Thirdly,* The *supreme power cannot take* from any man any part of his *property* without his own consent: for the preservation of property being the end of government, and that for which men enter into society, it necessarily supposes and requires, that the people should *have property,* without which they must be supposed to lose that, by entering into society, which was the end for which they entered into it; too gross an absurdity for any man to own. *Men* therefore *in society having property,* they have such a right to the goods, which by the law of the community are their's, that no body hath a right to take their substance or any part of it from them, without their own consent: without this they have no *property* at all; for I have truly no *property* in that, which another can by right take from me, when he pleases, against my consent. Hence it is a mistake to think, that the *supreme* or *legislative power* of any common-wealth, can do what it will, and dispose of the estates of the subject *arbitrarily,* or take any part of them at pleasure. This is not much to be feared in governments where the *legislative* consists, wholly or in part, in assemblies which are variable, whose members, upon the dissolution of the assembly, are subjects under the common laws of their country, equally with the rest. But in governments, where the *legislative* is in one lasting assembly always in being, or in one man, as in absolute monarchies, there is danger still, that they will think themselves to have a distinct interest from the rest of the community; and so will be apt to increase their own riches and power, by taking what they think fit from the people: for a man's *property* is not at all secure, tho' there be good and equitable laws to set the bounds of it between him and his fellow subjects, if he who commands those subjects have power to take from any private man, what part he pleases of his *property,* and use and dispose of it as he thinks good.

§. 139. But *government,* into whatsoever hands it is put, being, as I have before shewed, intrusted with this condition, and for *this end,* that men might have and secure their *properties;* the prince, or senate, however it may have power to make laws, for the regulating of *property* between the subjects one amongst another, yet can never have a power to take to themselves the whole, or any part of the subjects *property,* without their own consent: for this would be in effect to leave them no *property* at all. And to let us see, that even *absolute power*, where it is necessary, is *not arbitrary* by being absolute, but is still limited by that reason, and confined to those ends, which required it in some cases to be absolute, we need look no farther than the common practice of martial discipline: for the preservation of the army, and in it of the whole common-wealth, requires an *absolute obedience* to the command of every superior officer, and it is justly death to disobey or dispute the most dangerous or unreasonable of them; but yet we see, that neither the serjeant, that could command a soldier to march up to the mouth of a cannon, or stand in a breach, where he is almost sure to perish, can command that soldier to give him one penny of his money; nor the *general*, that can condemn him to death for deserting his post, or for not obeying the most desperate orders, can yet, with all his *absolute power* of life and death, dispose of one farthing of that soldier's estate, or seize one jot of his goods; whom yet he can command any thing, and hang for the least disobedience; because such a blind obedience is necessary to that end, for which the commander has his power, *viz.* the preservation of the rest; but the disposing of his goods has nothing to do with it.

§. 140. It is true, governments cannot be supported without great charge, and it is fit every one who enjoys his share of the protection, should pay out of his estate his proportion for the maintenance of it. But still it must be with his own consent, *i.e.* the consent of the majority, giving it either by themselves, or their representatives chosen by them: for if any one shall claim a *power to lay* and levy *taxes* on the people, by his own authority, and without such consent of the people, he thereby invades the *fundamental law of property*, and subverts the end of government: for what property have I in that, which another may by right take, when he pleases, to himself?

§. 141. *Fourthly*, The *legislative cannot transfer the power of making laws* to any other hands: for it being but a delegated power from the people, they who have it cannot pass it over to others. The people alone can appoint the form of the common-wealth; which is by constituting the legislative, and appointing in whose hands that shall be. And when the people have said, We will submit to rules, and be governed by *laws* made by such men, and in such forms, no body else can say other men shall make *laws* for them; nor can the people be bound by any *laws*, but such as are enacted by those whom they have chosen, and authorized to make *laws* for them. The power of the *legislative*, being derived from the people by a positive voluntary grant and institution, can be no other than what that positive grant conveyed, which being only to make *laws*, and not to make *legislators*, the *legislative* can have no power to transfer their authority of making *laws*, and place it in other hands.

§. 142. These are the *bounds* which the trust, that is put in them by the society, and the law of God and nature, have *set to the legislative* power of every common-wealth, in all forms of government.

First, They are to govern by *promulgated established laws*, not to be varied in particular cases, but to have one rule for rich and poor, for the favourite at court, and the country man at plough.

Secondly, These *laws* also ought to be designed for no other end ultimately but *the good of the people.*

Thirdly, They must *not raise taxes* on the *property of the people, without the consent of the people,* given by themselves, or their deputies. And this properly concerns only such governments where the *legislative* is always in being, or at least where the people have not reserved any part of the legislative to deputies, to be from time to time chosen by themselves.

Fourthly, The *legislative* neither must *nor can transfer the power of making laws* to any body else, or place it any where, but where the people have.

Discussion Questions

1. What is the importance of private property within Locke's theory of government?

2. How does Locke imagine that his ideal commonwealth will be governed?

Sources

John Locke, *Second Treatise of Government*, ed. C.B. Macpherson, Indianapolis and Cambridge: Hackett Publishing Company, 1980.

D.A. Lloyd Thomas, *Locke on Government*, London: Routledge, 1995.

CHAPTER 14

Baron de Montesquieu
The Persian Letters

Rousseau
The Social Contract

MONTESQUIEU, *THE PERSIAN LETTERS*

Born in 1698 to a provincial aristocratic family, Montesquieu was sent to study outside of Paris at an institution renowned for its liberal and innovative curriculum before returning to Bordeaux in 1705 to study law. He moved to Paris a few years later, where he began to make the acquaintance of the leading literary and scientific figures of the time. Montesquieu showed the manuscript of *The Persian Letters* to his friend and mentor, Desmolets, in 1720. Desmolet cautioned Montesquieu about the repercussions of publishing it, but assured the young writer that it would sell. Anonymously published in Amsterdam a year later, the work instantly won fame and notoriety in France. Montesquieu, although he refused to admit his authorship, was soon recognized as having penned the letters. He became a coveted attendee of Paris' most famed intellectual salons and clubs and enjoyed the recognition of these circles and France's leading academic institutions throughout his life. He wrote another masterpiece a few years before his death, *The Spirit of the Laws,* in which he advocated relativistic political systems based on a country's geography, economy, and culture.

The Persian Letters narrates the adventures of two Persian travelers who journey to France and remain there between the years of 1711 and 1720. The two main characters discuss their impressions of Parisian life, often making biting criticisms of French society, religion, and customs. The book reflects the interest of Europeans in travel and exotic locations generated by the discovery of the New World, yet Montesquieu turned the typical travelogue on its head by making France the foreign and exotic focus of investigation. This innovation, along with the letter format, permitted Montesquieu to interrogate the most pressing philosophical concerns of Europeans in the early eighteenth century. Montesquieu was writing before the Enlightenment thinkers began to fully question the compatibility of scientific, rational thought and religion. However, the climate of religious intolerance that he had witnessed led him to level harsh criticisms against the Catholic Church and the king's policies. In the letters below, Montesquieu uses a critique of Islam to question the arbitrary nature of religious rules and the persecution of other faiths. He subtly rails against the revocation of the Edict of Nantes by Louis XIV in the last of the following letters by condemning the expulsion of various peoples from the Persian empire.

THE PERSIAN LETTERS

Montesquieu

LETTER XXIX

Rica to Ibben, at Smyrna

The pope is the head of the Christians; he is an old idol, revered by custom. At one time he was formidable even to princes, for he deposed them as readily as our magnificent sultans depose kings of Irimetta or Georgia. But they no longer fear him. He proclaims himself as the successor of one of the first Christians, called St. Peter; and it is a rich succession indeed, for he has immense treasures and a large country under his rule.

The bishops are administrators subordinate to him, and they have, under his authority, two very different functions. When assembled together they make, as he does, articles of faith. As individuals, their only function is to dispense with obedience to the law. For you should know that the Christian religion is burdened with a multitude of practices very difficult to follow, and as it is judged harder to fulfill these duties than to have bishops to dispense with them, the latter course has been followed in the interest of public utility. So, if someone does not wish to observe the Rhamazan, or prefers not to subject himself to the formalities of marriage, or wishes to break his vows, or to marry within prohibited bans, or sometimes even to get release from an oath, he has only to go to the bishop or the pope, who immediately grants dispensation.

The bishops do not make articles of faith of their own accord. There are multitudes of doctors, dervishes for the most part, who raise among themselves thousands of new religious questions; they are allowed to dispute for a long time, and the quarrel lasts until a decision comes to terminate it.

I can also assure you that there has never been a realm so prone to civil wars as that of Christ.

Those who publicize some novel proposition are at first called heretics. Each heresy is given a name, which is a rallying cry for those supporting it. But no one is a heretic unless he wishes to be, for he needs only to split the difference and to offer some subtle distinction to his accusers, and no matter what the distinction is, or whether it is intelligible or not, it renders a man pure as snow and worthy of being called orthodox.

What I have said is good only for France and Germany, for I have heard that in Spain and Portugal there are dervishes who do not understand a joke, and who have a man burned as if he were straw. Whoever falls into the hands of these men is fortunate only if he has always prayed to God with little bits of wood in hand, has worn two bits of cloth attached to two ribbons, and has sometimes been in a province called Galicia! Otherwise, the poor devil is really in trouble. Even though he swears like a pagan that he is orthodox, they may not agree, and burn him for a heretic. It is useless for him to submit distinctions, for he will be in ashes before they even consider giving him a hearing.

Other judges presume the innocence of the accused; these always presume him guilty. In doubt they hold to the rule of inclining to severity, evidently because they consider mankind as evil. On the other hand, however, they hold such a high opinion of men that they judge them incapable of lying, for they accept testimony from deadly enemies, notorious women, and people living by some infamous profession. In passing sentence, the judges pay those condemned a little compliment, telling them that they are sorry to see them so poorly dressed in their brimstone shirts, that the judges themselves are gentlemen who abhor bloodletting, and are in despair at having to condemn them. Then, to console themselves, they confiscate to their own profit all the possessions of these poor wretches.

Happy the land inhabited by the children of the prophets! There these sad spectacles are unknown. The holy religion brought by the angels trusts truth alone for its defense, and does not need these violent means for its preservation.

Paris, the 4th of the moon of Chalval, 1712

LETTER LXI

Usbek to Rhedi, at Venice

The other day, I went into a famous church called Notre Dame, and while I was admiring that superb edifice I had occasion to talk with an ecclesiastic who was also there out of curiosity. The conversation turned on the tranquillity of his profession. "Most people," he said to me, "envy the happiness of our condition", and they are right. However, there are some disadvantages, for although we are largely separated from the world, yet we are drawn into it on a thousand occasions. Thus we have a very difficult role to sustain.

"Worldly people are astonishing: they can suffer neither our censure nor our praise. If we try to reform them, they find us ridiculous; but if we approve, they regard us as men out of character. Nothing is as humiliating as the thought that you are scandalizing even the impious. And so we are obliged to be equivocal and to influence the libertines not by consistent action but by making them uncertain about how we will receive their observations. This requires great ability; the state of neutrality is a hard one. Worldly people who risk everything, who give in to all fancies, who follow or abandon them as they are successful or not, fare much better."

"And this is not all. We cannot maintain in the world that happy and peaceful way of life which everyone considers so desirable. As soon as we appear, we are forced into dispute. We are asked, for instance, to prove the value of prayer to a man who does not believe in God, or the necessity of fasting to someone who has always denied the immortality of the soul; the task is laborious, and there is no laughter on our side. Furthermore, we are constantly tormented by a desire to convert others to our opinions, for this is, as it were, the essence of our profession; yet it is as ridiculous as if Europeans worked to improve human nature by bleaching the skin of the Africans. We disturb the state and torment ourselves by trying to establish religious doctrines which are not at all fundamental; we resemble that conqueror of China who drove his subjects to revolt by insisting that they cut their hair and fingernails."

"There is danger even in our zeal to enforce the duties of our holy religion among those for whom we are responsible, and it cannot be accompanied by too much prudence. An emperor named Theodosius once put to the sword every inhabitant of a city, even the women and children. Appearing shortly afterward before a church, he found that a bishop named Ambrose had closed the doors to him as a sacrilegious murderer. That was a heroic action. But when the emperor, having finally made the penance that his crime required, was later admitted to the church and went to sit among the priests, that same bishop made him sit elsewhere. And that was the action of a fanatic, for in truth, excessive zeal should be avoided. What difference did it make either to religion or to the state whether this prince had or had not a place among the priests?"

Paris, the 1st of the moon of Rebiab I, 1714

LETTER LXXV

Usbek to Rhedi, at Venice

I must admit that I have not noticed among the Christians that lively faith in their religion which one finds in Mussulmans. With them there are great distances from profession to belief, from belief to conviction, and from conviction to practice. Their religion is less a subject of sanctification than a subject for dispute, which is open to everyone. Courtiers, soldiers, even women rise up against ecclesiastics, demanding that they prove to them what they have resolved not to believe. It is not that they have rationally so decided, or that they have taken the trouble to examine the truth or falsehood of the religion they reject; rather they are rebels, who have felt the yoke and thrown it off before learning what it is. Moreover, they are no more firm in their incredulity than in their faith; they live in an ebb and flow which carries them constantly between belief and disbelief. One of them once told me: "I believe in the immortality of the soul in periods of six months. My opinions depend entirely upon my body's constitution. According to the level of my animal spirits, the adequacy of my digestion, the rarity or heaviness of the air I breathe, or the solidity of the food I eat, I am alternately a Spinozist, a Socinian, a Catholic, an unbeliever, or a zealot. When the physician is close to my bed, the confessor has an advantage on me. I easily prevent religion from afflicting me when I am well, but I permit it to console me when I am ill. When I possess nothing more of earthly hope, religion comes and seizes me with its promises; I am pleased to surrender to it and to die on the side of hope."

Long ago the Christian princes freed all the slaves in their realms, because they said Christianity makes all men equal. It is true that this religious act was very useful to them, for by it they lessened the power of the nobles over the common people. Since then they have conquered lands where they have seen it was to their advantage to hold slaves, whom they have permitted to be bought and sold, forgetting that religious principle which once so deeply affected them. What can I say about this? The truth of one time is the error of another. Why should we not act like Christians? We were foolish to refuse settlements and easy conquests in pleasant climates, only because the water there was not sufficiently pure for bathing according to the dictates of the sacred Koran.

I give thanks to the all-powerful God, who sent his great prophet Hali, that I profess a religion which transcends all human interests and is as pure as the heavens from which it descended.

Paris, the 13th of the moon of Saphar, 1715

LETTER LXXXV

Usbek to Mirza, at Ispahan

You know, Mirza, that certain ministers of Shah Soliman formed the plan of requiring all Armenians in Persia either to leave the kingdom or become Mohammedans, thinking that our empire would remain polluted so long as it kept these infidels in its bosom.

That would have been the end of Persian greatness, had the counsels of blind devotion won out on that occasion.

It is not known how the project failed. Neither those who made the proposal, nor those who rejected it, realized the consequence of their decision; chance assumed the office of reason and policy and saved the empire from a peril greater than would have resulted from the loss of a battle and the capture of two cities.

By proscribing the Armenians, it is calculated that all the merchants and most of the country's artisans would have been wiped out in a single day. I am sure that the great Shah Abbas would rather have cut off both his arms than sign such an order; in exiling to the lands of the Mogul and the other Indian kings his most industrious subjects, he would have felt that he was giving them half of his realm.

The persecution of the Guebres by our zealous Mohammedans has forced them to leave in crowds for India and has deprived Persia of a hardworking people which, by its labor alone, was close to victory over the sterility of our soil.

Yet there remained to fanaticism a second blow to strike, that against our industry. The result was that the empire fell from within, bringing down with it, as a necessary consequence, that very religion which the zealots wished to strengthen.

If unprejudiced discussion were possible, I am not sure, Mirza, that it would not be a good thing for a state to contain several religions.

It is noticed that members of tolerated religions usually render more service to their country than do those of the dominant religion, because, cut off from the customary honors, they can distinguish themselves only by an opulence and wealth acquired by their labor alone, and often in the most difficult professions.

Furthermore, since all religions contain precepts that are socially useful, it is well that they be zealously observed; and what is better able to animate that zeal than a multiplicity of religions?

They are rivals who pardon nothing, and their jealousy extends to individuals. Each holds himself on guard, fearful of doing something which might dishonor his sect and expose it to the scorn and unpardonable censures of the other group.

Also, it is often observed that the introduction of a new sect into a state is the surest way to correct abuses in the old.

It is vain to say that it is not in the prince's interest to tolerate various religions in his realm. All the sects of the world assembled together would bring him no harm, for there is not one of them that does not prescribe obedience and preach submission.

I admit that history is filled with religious wars, but let us be careful here, for it is not the multiplicity of religions which has produced these wars, but the spirit of intolerance stirring those who believed themselves to be in a dominant position.

This is the proselytizing spirit which the Jews caught from the Egyptians, and which has passed from them, like a common epidemic disease, to the Mohammedans and Christians.

It is, in short, a kind of madness, the progress of which can be regarded only as a total. eclipse of human reason.

Finally, even if it were not inhumane to afflict another's conscience, and even if there did not result from such an act those bad effects which spring up by the thousands, it would still be foolish to advise it. Whoever would have me change my religion doubtlessly acts as he does because he would not change his, however he was forced; yet he finds it strange that I will not do something which he would not do himself, perhaps for the entire world.

Paris, the 26th of the moon of Gemmadi I, 1715

Discussion Questions

1. What kind of ideals does Montesquieu propose in place of the religious hypocrisy that he deplores?

2. What, in Montesquieu's view, are the consequences of policies of religious persecution and expulsion for the Persian empire, and implicitly, France?

Sources

Montesquieu, *The Persian Letters*, trans. George R. Healy, Indianapolis and Cambridge: Hackett Publishing Company, 1999.

Peter V. Conroy, Jr., *Montesquieu Revisited*, New York: Twayne Publishers, 1992.

ROUSSEAU, THE SOCIAL CONTRACT

Born in 1712 to a French protestant family in Geneva, the death of his mother and the exile of his father marked Rousseau for life. In 1728, Rousseau himself left the city rather than the face punishment for a petty offense, and found romance and refuge in the house of Madame de Warens in Annency, France. His departure from Geneva marked the beginning of a life-long struggle find steady employment and emotional fulfillment. He worked as a servant, a tutor, a music transcriber and a writer, and constantly sought the companionship and patronage of wealthy, older women. Possessed of a difficult temperament and plagued by insecurity, Rousseau frequently argued with his patrons and broke with friends. He also fathered several children with a poor and uneducated servant woman, all of whom he sent to an orphanage, claiming that the state was better equipped than he to raise them.

Around 1745, Rousseau began to earn recognition for his work. He had received little formal education during his youth in Geneva and instead, schooled himself under the tutelage of his first patroness, Madame de Warens. After moving to Paris, he met Diderot, who in turn introduced the young philosopher to Parisian intellectual life. Rousseau contributed several entries on music to Diderot's *Encyclopedia* while he continued his studies, turning to political theory. However, rather than embrace the currents of thought so popular among the leading intellectuals of French society, Rousseau attacked Enlightenment ideals in an essay competition that won him immediate recognition. He published other works, among them a comic opera and several other entries in the *Encyclopedia.* By the mid-1750s, Rousseau was writing *The Social Contract.* In the meantime, relationships with patronesses and peers foundered, and Rousseau broke with Diderot, Grimm, Voltaire, and others. With the publication of *The Social Contract* and *Emile* in 1762, Rousseau was forced into exile. Rousseau ended his life in poverty, writing feverishly to justify his ideas until his death in 1778.

In *The Social Contract,* Rousseau considered the relationship between individuals and the state. Arguing that people must relinquish their individual liberties for the good of society as a whole, Rousseau left open-ended how the ideal society would govern itself, opening his work to diverse interpretations. Rousseau also attacked the notion of representative democracy, preferring more direct participation. In the passages below, Rousseau explores the nature of the social compact, the sovereign, and the civil state.

THE SOCIAL CONTRACT

Jean Jacques Rousseau

Let us assume that men have reached the point where the obstacles to their self-preservation in the state of nature are too great to be overcome by the forces each individual is capable of exerting to maintain himself in that state. This original state can then no longer continue; and the human race would perish if it did not change its mode of existence.

Now, since men cannot engender new forces, but can only combine and direct those already in existence, their only means of self-preservation is to form by aggregation a sum of forces capable of overcoming all obstacles, to place these forces under common direction, and to make them act in concert.

This sum of forces can only arise from the concurrence of many; but the force and liberty of each man being the primary instruments of his own self-preservation, how can he pledge them without harming himself and neglecting the cares he owes his own person? This problem, in relation to my subject, may be expressed in the following terms: To find a form of association which defends and protects the person and property of each member with the whole force of the community, and where each, while joining with all the rest, still obeys no one but himself, and remains as free as before.' This is the fundamental problem to which the social contract provides the answer.

The clauses of this contract are so completely determined by the nature of the act that the slightest modification would render them null and void; so that, though they may never have been formally declared, they are everywhere the same, everywhere tacitly admitted and recognised, until the moment when the violation of the social compact causes each individual to recover his original rights, and to resume his natural liberty as he loses the conventional liberty for which he renounced it.

These clauses, rightly understood, can be reduced to the following only: the total alienation of each member, with all his rights, to the community as a whole. For, in the first place, since each gives himself entirely, the condition is equal for all; and since the condition is equal for all, it is in the interest of no one to make it burdensome to the rest.

Furthermore, since the alienation is made without reservations, the union is as perfect as possible, and no member has anything more to ask. For if the individuals retained certain rights, each, in the absence of any common superior capable of judging between him and the public, would be his own judge in certain matters, and would soon claim to be so in all; the state of nature would continue, and the association would necessarily become tyrannical or meaningless.

Finally, each individual, by giving himself to all, gives himself to no one; and since there is no member over whom you do not acquire the same rights that you give him over yourself, you gain the equivalent of all you lose, and greater force to preserve what you have.

If the social compact is stripped to its essentials, therefore, you will find that it can be reduced to the following terms: 'Each of us puts in common his person and all his powers under the supreme direction of the general will; and in our corporate capacity we receive each member as an indivisible part of the whole.'

In place of the private and particular person of each of the contracting parties, this act of association immediately produces an artificial and collective body, made up of as many members as there are voices in the assembly, and receiving from this same act its unity, its collective personality, its life and its will. The public person thus formed by the union of all the rest was formerly known as a *city,* and is now called a *republic* or *body politic;* when passive it is known to its members as the *state,* when active as the *sovereign,* and as a *power* when it is being compared with its fellows. The members are known collectively as the *people;* and individually they are called, as participants in the sovereign authority, *citizens,* and, as men owing obedience to the laws of the state, *subjects.* But these terms are often confused and mistaken for one another; it is enough to be able to distinguish between them when they are used with absolute accuracy.

THE SOVEREIGN

From the formula already given, it can be seen that the act of association involves a reciprocal engagement between the public and its individual members, and that each individual, by contracting, so to speak, with himself, finds himself under the following two-fold obligation: as a member of the sovereign to the individual members, and as a member of the state to the sovereign. But the principle of civil law which states that no one can make binding commitments to himself is not applicable in this case; for there is a great difference between assuming obligations towards yourself, and doing so toward a whole of which you are a part.

It is also to be observed that public deliberation which, because of the two-fold nature of their relationship, is able to obligate all subjects toward the sovereign, cannot, for the opposite reason, obligate the sovereign toward itself; and that in consequence it is contrary to the nature of the body politic for the sovereign to bind itself by a law it cannot break. Since its relationships can only be conceived under a single aspect, it remains in the position of an individual contracting with himself; from which it follows that there is not, and cannot be, any sort of fundamental law binding on the body of the people, not even the social contract. This does not mean that this body cannot perfectly well assume obligations toward others in so far as they do not deviate from this contract; for in relation to foreigners, it becomes a simple entity, an individual.

But the body politic or sovereign, since it owes its being solely to the sanctity of the contract, can never bind itself, even to foreigners, to do anything derogatory to this original act, such as to alienate some part of itself or to subject itself to another sovereign. To violate the act by which it exists would be to destroy itself; and that which is nothing produces nothing.

From the moment when a multitude is thus united as a body, no one of its members can be offended without attacking the body itself; still less can the body be offended without affecting its members. Thus duty and interest alike oblige the two contracting parties to assist one another; and the same individuals should try to combine all the advantages which depend on both aspects of this twofold relationship.

Now the sovereign, being composed merely of the individuals who are its members, has and can have no interest contrary to theirs; consequently the sovereign power has no need to guarantee the rights of its subjects, since it is impossible for the body to want to harm all its members; and we shall see later that it cannot harm any particular individual. The sovereign, by the very fact that it exists, is always everything it ought to be.

The same is not true, however, of the relation of the subjects to the sovereign; in spite of their common interests, there would be no assurance that they would fulfil their obligations unless means were found to guarantee their fidelity.

Actually each individual may, as a man, have a private will contrary to, or divergent from, the general will he has as a citizen. His particular interest may speak to him quite differently from the common interest; his existence, being naturally absolute and independent, may make him envisage his debt to the common cause as a gratuitous contribution, the loss of which will be less harmful to others than the payment is burdensome to himself; and regarding the artificial person of the state as a fictitious being, because it is not a man, he would like to enjoy the rights of a citizen without fulfilling the duties of a subject, an injustice which, if it became progressive, would be the ruin of the body politic.

In order, therefore, that the social compact may not be a meaningless formality, it includes the tacit agreement, which alone can give force to the rest, that anyone who refuses to obey the general will shall be forced to do so by the whole body; which means nothing more or less than that he will be forced to be free. For this is the condition which, by giving each citizen to his country, guarantees him against any form of personal dependence; it is the secret and the driving force of the political mechanism; and it alone gives legitimacy to civil obligations, which otherwise would be absurd, tyrannical, and subject to the gravest abuses.

THE CIVIL STATE

This passage from the natural to the civil state produces a very remarkable change in man, substituting justice for instinct as the guide to his conduct, and giving his actions the morality they previously lacked. Then only is it that the voice of duty takes the place of physical impulse, and law the place of appetite; and that man, who until then has thought only of himself, finds himself compelled to act on other principles, and to consult his reason before listening to his inclinations. Although in this state he loses many of his natural advantages, he gains so many in return, his faculties are exercised and developed, his ideas are broadened, his sentiments ennobled and his whole soul elevated to such an extent that if the abuses of this new condition did not often degrade him beneath his former state, he ought unceasingly to bless the happy moment which wrested him forever from it, and turned him from a stupid and limited animal into an intelligent being and a man.

Let us draw up the balance sheet in terms readily capable of comparison. What man loses by the social contract is his natural liberty, and an unlimited right to everything he wants and is capable of getting; what he gains is civil liberty, and the ownership of all he possesses. In order to make no mistake as to the balance of profit and loss, we must clearly distinguish between natural liberty, which has no other limit than the might of the individual, and civil liberty, which is limited by the general will; and between possession, which results merely from force or from the right of the first occupier, and property, which can only be founded on a positive title.

To the foregoing we might add that, along with the civil state, man acquires moral liberty, which alone makes him truly master of himself; for the impulse of mere appetite is slavery, and obedience to self-imposed law is liberty. But I have already said more than enough under this head, and the philosophic meaning of the word liberty is not my present subject.

Discussion Questions

1. What kinds of rights and obligations does Rousseau envision the individual would possess in an ideal society?

2. How would you characterize Rousseau's ideal society? Were his intentions to create a more democratic or a more authoritarian society?

Sources

Jean Jacques Rousseau, *Political Writings*, trans. Frederick Watkins, Madison: University of Wisconsin Press, 1953.

Robert Wokler, *Rousseau: A Very Short Introduction*, Oxford and New York: Oxford University Press, 2001.

CREDITS

From *Gilgamesh,* translated by John Gardner and John Maier. Copyright © 1984 by Estate of John Gardner and John Maier. Used by permission of Alfred A. Knopf, a division of Random House, Inc.

From *The Ancient Egyptian Book of the Dead,* translated by Raymond O. Faulkner, Carol Andrews, ed. Copyright © 1972 The Limited Editions Club, New York, Revised edition 1985.

From Herodotus, *The Histories of Herodotus of Halicarnassus,* translated by Harry Carter. Copyright © 1958 by The George Macy Companies, Inc.

From Plato, *Apology of Socrates,* translated by Michael C. Stokes. Copyright © 1997 M.C. Stokes. Reprinted by permission of Aris & Phillips Ltd.

From Arrian, *The Life of Alexander the Great*, translated by Aubrey de Selincourt. Copyright © 1958 Aubrey de Selincourt. Reprinted with permission of Penguin Putnam Ltd.

From *The Aeneid of Virgil* by Allen Mandelbaum. Copyright © 1971 by Allen Mandelbaum. Used by permission of Bantam Books, a division of Random House.

From *The Works of Josephus,* translated by William Whiston. Peabody, Mass.: Hendrickson Publishers, 1987. Used by permission of the publisher.

From Egeria, *Diary of a Pilgrimage*, translated by George E. Gingras in *Ancient Christian Writers, The Works of the Fathers in Translation*, No. 38, edited by Johannes Quasten, Walter J. Burghardt, Thomas Comerford Lawler. Copyright © 1970 by Rev. Johannes Quasten, Rev. Walter J. Burghardt, S.J., and Thomas Comerford Lawler. Used with permission of Paulist Press.

From Ibn Ridwan, *Medieval Islamic Medicine, Ibn Ridwan's Treatise "On the Prevention of Bodily Ills in Egypt,"* translated by Michael W. Dols, edited by Adil S.Gamal, in *Comparative Studies of Health Systems and Medical Care*, edited by Charles Leslie. Copyright © 1984 by The Regents of the University of California Press. Reprinted by permission of University of California Press.

From Einhard, *The Life of Charlemagne,* translated by Evelyn Scherabon Firchow and Edwin H. Zeydel. Copyright © 1972 by University of Miami Press. Reprinted by permission of University of Miami Press.